From High School to Prison: Apply Your Hustle Differently and End Better Than You Start

By Ronnie Hicks

© 2021 Ronnie Hicks

All rights reserved. This book or any portion thereof may not be reproduced or used in any manner whatsoever without the express written permission of the publisher except for the use of brief quotations in a book review or scholarly journal.

First Edition: July 2021

From High School to Prison: Apply Your Hustle Differently and End Better Than You Start/ By Ronnie Hicks

ISBN: **978-1-943616-43-5**

Publisher: MAWMedia Group, LLC

Los Angeles | Reno | Nashville

> People usually graduate and go to the Workforce, Military, or College. I went to Prison. Learn from what happened to me.

DEDICATION

I would like to dedicate this book to my mother, my father, my grandparents, my kids, my brothers, and my entire family and friends. Special shoutout to my hood UpEast, my city Bennettsville, and the whole Marlboro County. North Carolina as a whole, much love to the whole state and everyone I met on my journey. Thank you all for helping me write my life story.

Table of Contents

- Section I: Street Life 8
- Chapter 1: Knee Deep 9
- Chapter 2: Street Life 18
- Chapter 3: After High School 23
- Chapter 4: Crime and Time 34
- Section II: Being Honest with Myself 60
- Chapter 5: Time on My Hands 61
- Chapter 6: More Work to Do 69
- Chapter 7: Reading and Learning and Growing 86
- Chapter 8: Trust Issues 95
- Section III: Investment 111
- Chapter 9: Investment in Self 112
- Chapter 10: Investment in Your Business 118
- Chapter 11: Investment in People 143

Section I: Street Life

Chapter 1: Knee Deep

My Hood was called UpEast. Everything was cool through elementary school and junior high school. High school was a different story. Our whole county, Marlboro, attends the same high school. All these small towns came together into one high school. Each of these towns and neighborhoods had their own identity. The tradition through the generations was to beef with other neighborhoods as a matter of pride. It was not a matter of gangs. It was just neighborhood and town beef.

High School

We used to roll deep when it was time to go hit the parties and the high school dances. We always had beef with somebody, or somebody always had beef with us. Up East Boys was a neighborhood thing. Fights were common. Prior to school, during school, after school, we would find places to fight and air out our grievances. It was always about little stuff, most often a girl.

Kev was my right-hand man. I remember taking him to see this girl he hooked up with at school from Clio South Carolina. I thought it was crazy how we use to beef with them boys from Clio and go to their town to holla at their girls. We be at school about to kill each other, then we roll in their hood to get at their girls.

We was some wild boys. Those trips to Clio, resulted in fatherhood for me at 15 years old. Instantly, I was a kid with a kid on the way. Still in High School. Still living with my parents. Still knee deep in the streets.

I lived on Cook Street growing up. Cook Street is the main street that ran through my hood. My house was the house where all the kids in the hood liked to hangout. From our location, you could see everybody come through the hood. I never forget how they had my street labeled one bad street to drive on at night.

We were out of control. We threw rocks at people's cars who were driving down the street at night. We thought it was fun. We saw it as just being kids, but things got serious when somebody threw a brick and hit this white lady in the face while she was driving. I will never forget that night, I still can hear how she slammed on breaks. We all took off running. Next thing you know, the police pulled up on everybody's house. We were all in trouble. The whole hood went to court behind that night.

From Highschool to Prison

Homes in the Hood

My brothers and I were the only ones who grew up with a mom and a dad in their home. That did not make a difference in the choices we made, but it was a difference for us. Some of them had stepfathers, but only a handful had both parents. The result was a difference in the level of correction and discipline that was modeled in my neighborhood. A man discipline differently. Their example is an influence that pours something positive into a male child.

My dad was a DJ prior to my birth. He provided for us the best he could. He was strict on us because he knew that were many distractions in the street life. He would always remind us that we will not end up in jail or dead. He did not allow us to stay out past the streetlamp lighting. He also would tell us to stay in the yard during certain times. He kept us grounded. I still did what I did, but I knew to keep it from him as much as possible.

My grandad was a chef, so my father cooked most of the time. My parents did their best as parents. It was the environment that got the best of me. If you are not careful, you can make choices that get you caught up. You may want to be in the in-crowd contrary to the guidance of your parents. Especially in the context of social media today, the pressure to be like others is stronger than ever. The results are rarely good.

My Older Brothers

My oldest brother was shot over a girl situation. He lived. I was in high school when that happened. The shooter did not get any time because of the shooting. I really wanted to retaliate, but my brothers and I decided against vengeance.

My brothers had the lifestyle of the hood famous complete with the finest clothes, shoes, and other status symbols. I listened to Cash Money and that lifestyle of getting money. Music, along with the influence of my brothers, caused me to gravitate to that lifestyle. I shopped out of town to get things that people in my hometown in South Carolina would not have.

I was way ahead of my time. I got my driver license at 15 years old. My main man Kev and I were getting all the girls. We were UP EAST teenagers catching the Amtrak and Greyhound buses to New York just to go shopping and visit his family.

From Highschool to Prison

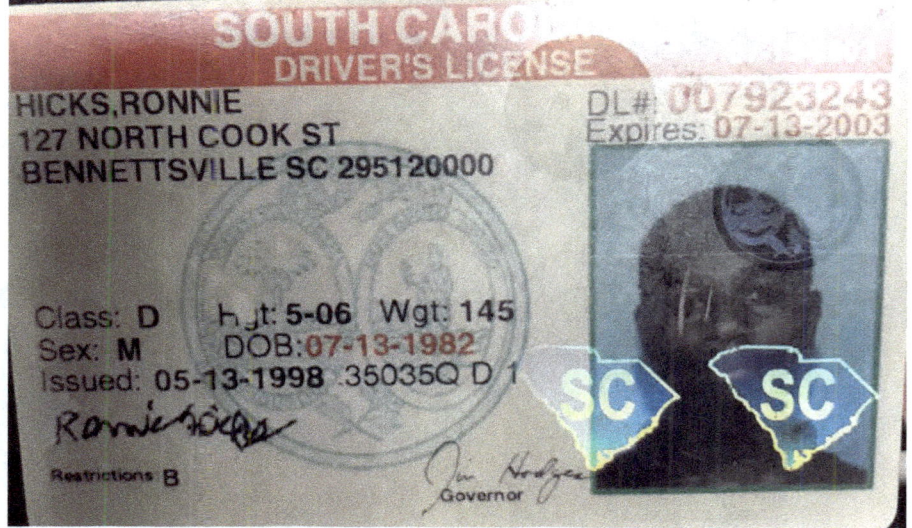

As the youngest of five boys, I had an advantage over other kids. I had my father as an example who knew the streets. I had two older brothers who taught me about the current street life. Everyone was into music especially on my dad's side of the family. This was back when the herring-bone chains, gold teeth, and 80s hip hop was huge. One of my brothers was a local rapper. My cousin grew to be Fantasia—winner of American Idol's third season.

I got into hustling just as a natural activity of my neighborhood. My brothers did a little something, but we never really talked about that. I was just doing my thing and providing for myself.

From Highschool to Prison

From Highschool to Prison

Chapter 2: Street Life

Hustling weed in school, crack on the street. Drug classes. It was an NA. It was not about offering another alternative to street life.

The year 2000, the month of May was my last month in High School as a senior. Around this time everybody is hyped up about graduation and going to college to further their education. I was the last to finish school out of five boys in my household and I use to wonder how that made my dad feel to see his boys go through high school since he dropped out at an early age. I was street smart and book smart also athletic. I wanted to play sports I tried out, but I hated staying after school. I always felt like I was missing something in the streets, so I quit.

The Fruit of Street Life

Running the streets with the neighborhood drug dealers, I became a product of my environment. I started hustling around the age of 14. I

From Highschool to Prison

was a smart hustler, clean cut, and low key. I handled my business mostly by myself or with only one of my partners. I never let the streets take me off getting my education. I used my book smarts during the day and my street smarts at night.

My son was born on January 13, 1999 I was only 16 years old. I continued working my way out of High School. I knew it was time to provide for this child, but all I ever knew was hustle in them streets. I tried to get jobs, but again I felt like I was missing something in the streets. I even got a job at an amusement park during the Summer. I ended up quitting that job when one of my co-workers put me up on selling tickets. I used to make money by buying stolen tickets for wholesale. I would sell them retail to the families arriving at the park before they had a chance to purchase at the gate. I would give them a better deal than they would get if they paid at the gate. I found myself hustling at the amusement park just like I use to in my hood. It was a great hustle until the security guard caught on to me and kicked me off the premises. I remember the pressure I put on myself. In my mind, I had to go extra hard because my son's first Christmas was coming up. His birthday was a couple weeks after Christmas.

When my son first Christmas came around, he was straight. I went to the outlet stores in Conway S.C. and got him everything. Whenever his mom said he needed something, I made sure he had it. I used to pick him up after he turned one year old and let him hang out with me. I remember putting him in the front seat and putting the seat belt on him like he was grown. I did not know better. I didn't care about a car seat. My son and I were just rolling around town chilling listening to cash money and No Limit cd's. After one of our days chilling, I forgot to check him over and dropped him off to his mom. She blanked on me for dropping him off with his diaper messed up.

Busted

I remember sitting in my math class about to sell some weed to a classmate and noticed one of the guys that monitor the hallways come inside the class asking my teacher can he pull me out of class for a minute. He told me to bring my bookbag, I told him it was in my locker. Once I walked out into the hallway, I noticed my boy Kev standing by the door. The hall monitor asked that I take him to my locker. By this time, I'm looking at Kev for the what's up, but I can't say much. I get to my locker, and the hall monitor is on some search and seizure tip. He goes through my bookbag, I know what time it is now. Somebody snitching on me and my man Kev. The hall monitor then speaks to us in abrupt tones after finding nothing in my locker. "Let's go to the office."

The whole time I got a few bags of weed in my pocket. My mind is racing knowing I can't walk into the office with this weed on me. I happen to see one of my boys hanging out the gym door as we were walking by. I tossed the bag towards him on the low, but the hall monitor saw the bag hit the floor out of the corner of his eye. He picked it up with a flourish like he had just won the lottery. "This what we been looking for."

"That's not mine. You found that on the floor!" He was not amused by my ruse.

When we walked into the office, I saw police officers and a guy I sold to earlier that day. They told him to leave. They searched me and Kev. Kev had a few nickel bags behind his belt. They did not find them. They let him go. The hall monitor grinned like a Cheshire cat at the cops while gesturing toward me. "Look at what I found on Mr. Hicks."

I repeated my defense. "Man, you got that off the floor!" No support. They called my dad and they suspended me, and I could not come back to school unless I took a drug class. I was assigned to such a class and scheduled for attendance.

My dad was hot at me. "You always stay in something." I was his baby boy, but he didn't play no games with us. Thinking back when I was younger and I did something wrong, my dad would say, "Take off them clothes." He would beat us with drop cords, belts, or whatever he could get his hands on. He was cool to the kids in the hood. Everybody liked my dad because he was like the go to man if you need your bike fixed or your go cart supped up. He was mechanically inclined and a favorite Mr. Fixit.

My mom was more of a homebody. She did not get out much. My dad did everything from cooking to planting all kinds of fruit trees in the backyard and doing yard work. He did all this while working a job. My mom was real laid back and soft spoken. My dad used to drink a lot and smoke cigarettes all the time. I feel like I took my mom side in some ways. Mom did not drink or smoke. I don't drink or smoke. I am also laid back. After completing the drug class, I went back to school. I knew who told on me, but I never said nothing. I just cut him off.

Chapter 3: After High School

All throughout my High School years, I was a popular kid. I had a mouth full of white gold teeth, gold and diamond rings, Cubin link gold chain with a gold and diamond cut with a Mary charm hanging from it. I used to have a new pair of shoes every week and stayed with some new clothes. Everybody called me "Cool Daddy," but when No Limit and Master P hit the scene, they started calling me "Silk." They said I looked like Silkk Da Shocker. Some people said I was smooth like silk. I used to kick it with all the girls. They all liked me in their own way.

There was one particular girl that I was feeling. She and I got up one night when I borrowed my aunt's car. I went to pick her up and we drove to the lakeside. We both got in the backseat to make out but as soon as we were about to get heavy, the car started rolling back towards the water. I was parked on a hill and my aunt car was not a good car to park on a hill without the emergency break up. I reacted quick as a whip and grabbed the wheel from the backseat and turned it from going into the water and the car backed into a ditch. The front end of the car was looking up at the sky. That was so embarrassing. I had to run up the hill to my cousin house to use the phone. I called my brother and a few more people to help me get the car out of the ditch.

Tragedies

In my senior year in school with only a week until graduation day, tragedy struck. I'm rolling through my hood and I see one of my boys trying to get my attention to pull over. I asked him what was up. "You didn't hear the news?"

"What news?"

"Tip got killed in a car accident." I couldn't believe what I was hearing, Tip was my girlfriend back in 7th and 8th grade we broke up when she went to High School, but we were still close friends. All I could think about is the last time I saw her. It was about a week ago at her grandmother's house. We were laughing and having a good time. I never knew that was going to be the last time I would see her alive. She was like my first love in Middle School.

From Highschool to Prison

Around this time my dad was in and out the hospital. He was a diabetic, and he loved to drink beer and smoke cigarettes. The doctor said he needed to let go of the smoking and drinking; I remember him having to go to the rest home for old people though he was only 49 years old.

My dad called me from the nursing home asking me to bring a soda and a pack of Marlboro Cigarettes. I purchased the soda but not the cigarettes because the Doc said he should not be smoking. When I got to the rest home he asked, "Where my cigarettes?"

"I didn't buy them because you don't need to be smoking." He took the drink and walked away upset at me. I left.

A few days later, I got a call from my aunt saying my dad just passed away. My heart dropped and tears just started falling. Again, I did not know that my last encounter would be the last time I would see my father alive. I couldn't breathe. I tried to tell my brothers, but I couldn't even get it out.

I couldn't believe this was happening a week before the class of 2000 graduation. I just loss a friend and two days later my dad passed away. This marked a moment in time when everything started going downhill for me, I no longer had that man to get on me when I did wrong. I had to attend two funerals and I had a graduation day in a few days.

Downhill Ignoring the Signs

After graduation, everybody went to the beach to celebrate our achievement. The celebration took a lot off my mind. The next morning, me and my boys went to eat breakfast together. We ate good that morning and all ate for free. We got full and walked out one by one.

From Highschool to Prison

That Summer was long. I was dating a girl I was really feeling. She was a virgin. I was not, of course. I was already a father. I was still seeing my old High School sweetheart, but things were not the same between us after her mom forced her to have an abortion. We were still cool though. She lived around the block from my boy's girlfriend, so I would see her from time to time when I ride out that way with my boy.

Me and Tim were really close like me and Kev. I knew Tim since first grade. He was my next-door neighbor, so we really grew up together. We started moving work together from NC to SC. We were out of school and didn't have anything but time on our hands. The streets were all we knew, and they paid well.

My brother had the perfect spot across the bypass for us to set up shop. Me, Tim, and Kev moved our operation across town to multiply our money. My cousin was known across the bypass, but he was a crackhead. A crackhead, but not your average crackhead. He handled a lot of business for me so I could keep a low profile. As long as I took care of him, he was reliable. He never crossed me because I did right by him.

One night while making a sale, his life flashed right before my eyes. The car that he was serving tried to snatch the work from him and he grabbed the driver. The driver pulled off dragging my cousin. The car soon ran into a ditch just missing a house. I saw my cousin limping toward me with a message. "Leave the block. It's about to get hot." I got him in the car with me to make sure he was good, and I took off.

My boy Kev ended up hitting a lick for some bad work. We tried to move it, but they wanted that fire I usually have. We was losing customers because I had to wait on my people to reup. I had to take that trip to NC to holla at my people to get my customers what they wanted.

That story is the beginning of a choice to go downhill. My boy Tim was dealing with this girl from the sandhills that had a wild but cool cousin named Dee. I always knew Dee, but I never hung with him like that. When Tim was not with me, he was in the sandhills with Dee. I didn't know that he and Dee would hook up to hit a lick.

Tim showered me with the story like it was the best Christmas ever. "We hit a sweet lick, Silk. You really should get down with us." Being a stick-up kid wasn't my thing. I liked to hustle. I would like to think that it was a choice based on morals or principles, but it was just outside my experience. Welcome to Training Day. This one night, I was chilling with Dee and Tim. They were talking about a lick that got my attention. It is always the promise of the come up that entices a hustler. That was the day I became a stick-up kid. I was not really thinking at all. I was just wilding out and getting money however I could get it.

From Highschool to Prison

We made plans to go to Fayetteville. Before we left SC, I remember my boy mom telling him to stay home. "Don't leave." She pleaded with him as we waited on him. She must have had a feeling about what was about to go down. We all left anyway. Me, Tim, Lance, and Dee. Lance was Tim's cousin—laid back, good dude, down for whatever.

We ended up in Hamlet, NC before we headed to Fayetteville. We stopped by this store that was open late. All our minds were thinking the same thing. Let's rob this spot. I did not go in, but I knew the other two were going in to pull a job. I knew I was not on any cameras.

On our way to Fayetteville, out of all cars, we were pulled over. I don't remember why we pulled over. The police flashed their lights and motioned for us to pull to the side of the road. We complied. My mind was on the fact that we had not made it to Fayetteville, and we were about to go to jail. We had just robbed a store. We had bullets and guns in the car. It was over before it really started. The officer took the driver's ID and went back to his car. We sat silently in the car as if talking would give away our secret. The officer came back to the car, said all is well, and allowed us to go without a citation. That was another sign that we should reconsider our plans. After the officer let us go, we kept riding. We didn't think to go back to SC. Our mission was set. So too was our fate.

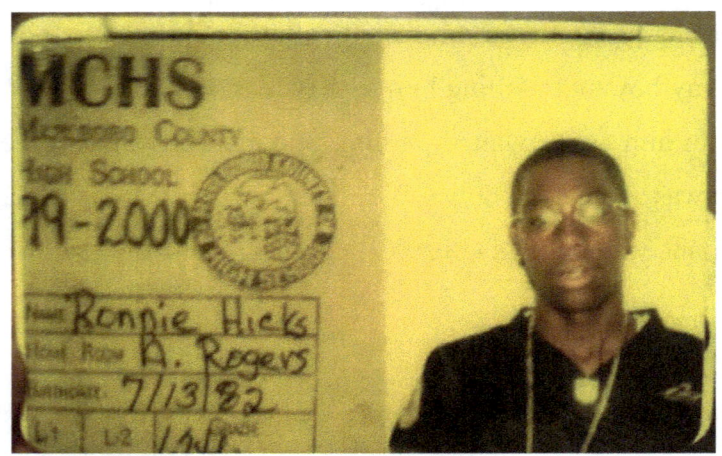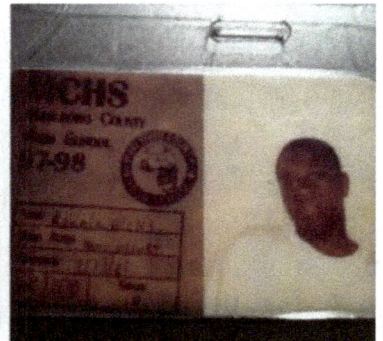

From Highschool to Prison

From Highschool to Prison

Chapter 4: Crime and Time

We got in Fayetteville around 6:00am that morning. We commenced to joy riding and looking for something or somebody to rob. We ended up breaking into cars that looked nice. We cared about nothing.

Around 9:00am that morning, we saw this dope boy driving his GS300 Lexus on 22's. Assuming he got money or drugs on him, we followed him to this pawn shop he owned. As soon as he got out of the car, me and Dee ran up on him with a .40 pistol. I took the keys, and Dee held the burner on him. We jumped in the whip and took off.

Lance and Tim followed behind me, I drove maybe half a mile down the road and the whole car shut down. The steering wheel locked up, and the car just cut off. I didn't immediately comprehend what was happening, but I knew time was up on this car. Lance and Tim swerved in front of me. We hopped out and left the car in the middle of the street.

From Highschool to Prison

Come to find out, the car was equipped with a remote kill switch. That would be devastating, but that's not the only information we would find out. Following us, in another car, was the owner of the car. He had activated the remote kill switch to shut his car down and alerted the police. Now, we were the prey, four deep in Lance's car being trailed by a man determined not to be a victim. Among our miscalculations that morning, we were prevented from leaving Fayetteville because the early morning traffic was crazy.

We made it to Bragg Blvd, but no farther. What appeared to me like 50 police cars were coming straight towards us from the front and another 50 behind us. We got guns and bullets in the car along with stolen goods we had pilfered earlier. We were trapped. There was no way out of this. Lance made a complete stop. The police then sprang from their cars with guns pointed "Get out of the car one by one."

Dee wanted to shoot it out with them, but I wasn't with that. For one, we were outnumbered. For two, we didn't have that many bullets. One of the officers yelled, "Driver, cut the car off put the keys out the window. Get out with your hands up." Lance turned the engine off and was the first to surrender and get out. The officers yelled for me to get out next from the passenger side. They ran up and forced me to the ground, cuffed me, and threw me in the back of a patrol car with no back seat just hard plastic.

That was my last day on the streets. Just that fast, I was put away not thinking at all about what I was doing or how I was living. I couldn't shake the plea being repeated in my head. "I am not a stick-up kid. I'm a hustler." I made thousands of dollars hustling and was good at it. I never got caught while hustling. Stepping outside of my norm got me caught up.

County Jail

By the time my mind again registered the present, we were all sitting in the Cumberland County Jail with a high bond. We knew that bailing out was not worth a hope. Nobody was putting up their house for collateral to bail us out. The detectives split us up and took us to our cells. Tim's cell was right beside my cell. We talked every day. Lance and Dee were on the other side of the jail. Tim snuck in some cigarette tobacco, and everybody was happy to know he had something for them to smoke. He had taken the tobacco out of the cigarettes before we changed into our jumpsuits. I do not know where he hid it, but he was thinking ahead. Those boys smoked those with rolled bible pages from the free bibles in the jail.

Everybody in the cellblock was cool. We never had a problem with nobody. They found out we were from South Carolina and started calling us "South Click." I remember making that collect call to my fam to tell them I was locked up. I also had to call my son's mother. When I did, she said something that cut through me like a knife. "You didn't take the time out to think about your son?" Knowing I didn't think about him, I was at a loss for words.

Everybody looked forward to visitation and mail call in the county jail. You find out real fast who really cares about you when you find yourself behind bars. I had a few people to come visit me at the county jail and send me letters, but the ones you think will be there for you are the ones that go missing.

Time passed like turtles crossing a country road while I sat in this backwoods jail waiting to go to court. Tensions started to rise. Everyone in the cell block found something to get mad about so they could fight. It got to a point that when the officers brought a new inmate no one knew into our cell block, somebody will set it off on him. Everybody would jump on him just because. We got so bad that we were in competition with the cellblock my boy Tim was in. We fought to see who could send the new inmates to ICU the fastest. My block was so bad that the warden came to visit with a request. "If you're good for a week and keep the cell block clean, I will order Papa John's pizza every week." The reward was enough to broker peace. Everybody chilled out. That pizza each week was manna to a sojourning mass of misguided men. We used to look forward to that pizza.

Adding Time

One day while lying on my bunk, I get called out my cell for an unexpected visit that wasn't on visitation day. As the guard walked me to the visiting room, my mind raced. I had not requested a special visit. I wondered who the visitor could be. Soon as I walked into the room, I see two sheriff deputies from my hometown. My mind shifted immediately. Now, I'm thinking, *Why would they be coming here to N.C. to see me all the way from Bennettsville, SC?* When I took a seat, they told me they been working with Richmond County police.

"We feel like you and your co-defendants were involved in some other robberies."

From Highschool to Prison

"I don't know what you're talking about. You got the wrong one." They pointed out that they had a surveillance tape of a robbery that took place at a convenience store in Richmond county. One of the officers said they checked our personal belongings and found a marked two-dollar bill in my co-defendant property. Even though I wasn't on camera, they were going to link me to this robbery. They told me they were going back to my mom's house in S.C. and search my car. They took my car keys out of my property and illegally searched my car. Once I got back to my cell, I holla at Tim. He spilled that the investigators questioned all of us.

Getting a visit about facing more charges was the last thing I needed. I stayed in the county jail for nine months. I was the last one to leave out of my co-defendants. I woke up in jail on my 19th birthday July 13th, 2001 to an officer rousing me for a court appearance that day. When I entered the courtroom, I was alone. Nobody was in there that I knew, no family no so-called homeboys from the hood, no girls I spent money on or dated, nobody.

It was my birthday. I'm thinking the judge already knew this. I thought he might take it easy on me. Little did I know he couldn't care less. I was sentenced to prison still facing more charges. It was a letdown for sure. Certainly, it was not the birthday that I would have hoped for. Not the reception I had in my mind.

I was transferred the next day to prison. Prison the day after my 19th birthday. it felt good seeing the sun light and getting out of that county jail after 9 months. As they loaded us up on the bus, I just enjoyed the little bit of fresh air outside while it lasted. 19 years old on my way to the big house and left my son Shaliek fatherless at the age of one.

North Carolina Department of Correction
Public Access Information System

Instructions: Here is the information you have requested for this offender.
(Note: Click here to view an Explanation of Terms and Data Elements used in the summary boxes.)

Data current as of: 02/28/2002

General Summary Information

DOC Number: 0732127
Inmate Status: ACTIVE

Name(s): HICKS, RONNIE

Demographics

Gender:	MALE	Body Build:	MEDIUM
Race:	BLACK	Complexion:	DARK
Age:	19	Birth Date:	07/13/1982
Height:	6' 0"	Weight:	147 lbs
Hair:	BLACK	Eyes:	BROWN
Citizenship:	BORN IN U.S.		
Ethnic:	AFRICAN		
Primary Language:			
NC County of Birth:	OTHER		
Country of Birth:	UNITED STATES		

Most Recent Incarceration Summary

Conviction Date: 07/13/2001
Projected Release Date: 07/19/2004
Crime: ROBBERY W/DANGEROUS WEAPON (PRINCIPAL)
Admission Date: 07/18/2001
Special Characteristics: REGULAR
Custody Classification: MEDIUM
Control Status: REGULAR POPULATION

Total Term: 5 YEARS 3 MONTHS
Crime Type: FELON
Admitting Location: POLK YI
Next Custody Review Date: 02/07/2002
Next Control Review: UNKNOWN

From Highschool to Prison

Sentence Number: BA-001
Conviction Date: 07/13/2001
Service Status: EXPIRED
Punishment Type: ACTIVE SS
Sentence Type 1: DEPT OF CCFR DIV OF PRISONS
Minimum Term: 3 YEARS 9 MONTHS

Commitment Type: INMATE
County Of Conviction: CUMBERLAND
Sentence Begin Date: 07/13/2001
Actual Release Date: 07/19/2004
Projected Release Date: 07/19/2004
Maximum Term: 5 YEARS 3 MONTHS

Commitment	Docket#	Offense (Qualifier)	Offense Date	Type	Sentencing Penalty Class Code
INITIAL	00043608	ROBBERY W/DANGEROUS WEAPON (PRINCIPAL)	10/23/2000	FELON	CLASS D
CONSOLIDATED FOR JUDGMENT	00043605	LARCENY (OVER $200) (PRINCIPAL)	10/19/2000	FELON	CLASS H
CONSOLIDATED FOR JUDGMENT	00043608	ROBBERY W/DANGEROUS WEAPON (CONSPIRACY)	10/23/2000	FELON	CLASS E

Sentence Number: BA-002
Conviction Date: 02/14/2002
Service Status: EXPIRED
Punishment Type: POST RELEASE
Sentence Type 1: DEPT OF CORR DIV OF PRISONS
Sentence Type 3: POST RELEASE SENTENCE
Minimum Term: 6 YEARS 10 MONTHS
Parole Begin Date: 12/09/2008

Commitment Type: INMATE
County Of Conviction: RICHMOND
Sentence Begin Date: 02/14/2002
Actual Release Date: 12/09/2008
Projected Release Date: 12/09/2008
Maximum Term: 9 YEARS
Parole End Date: 09/05/2009

Commitment	Docket#	Offense (Qualifier)	Offense Date	Type	Sentencing Penalty Class Code
CONCURRENT TO SENTENCE NUMBER BA-001	01005449	ROBBERY W/DANGEROUS WEAPON (PRINCIPAL)	10/23/2000	FELON	CLASS D
CONSOLIDATED FOR JUDGMENT	01005450	ROBBERY W/DANGEROUS WEAPON (PRINCIPAL)	10/23/2000	FELON	CLASS D

(1)

From: your mother
To: Ronnie   3-2-05

Hello Ronnie,
How you doing? OK I hope.

Ronnie Hicks
Wake Correctional
1000 Rock Quarry Rd.
Raleigh, N.C. 27610

who got killed a couple of month
Iraq,

From Highschool to Prison

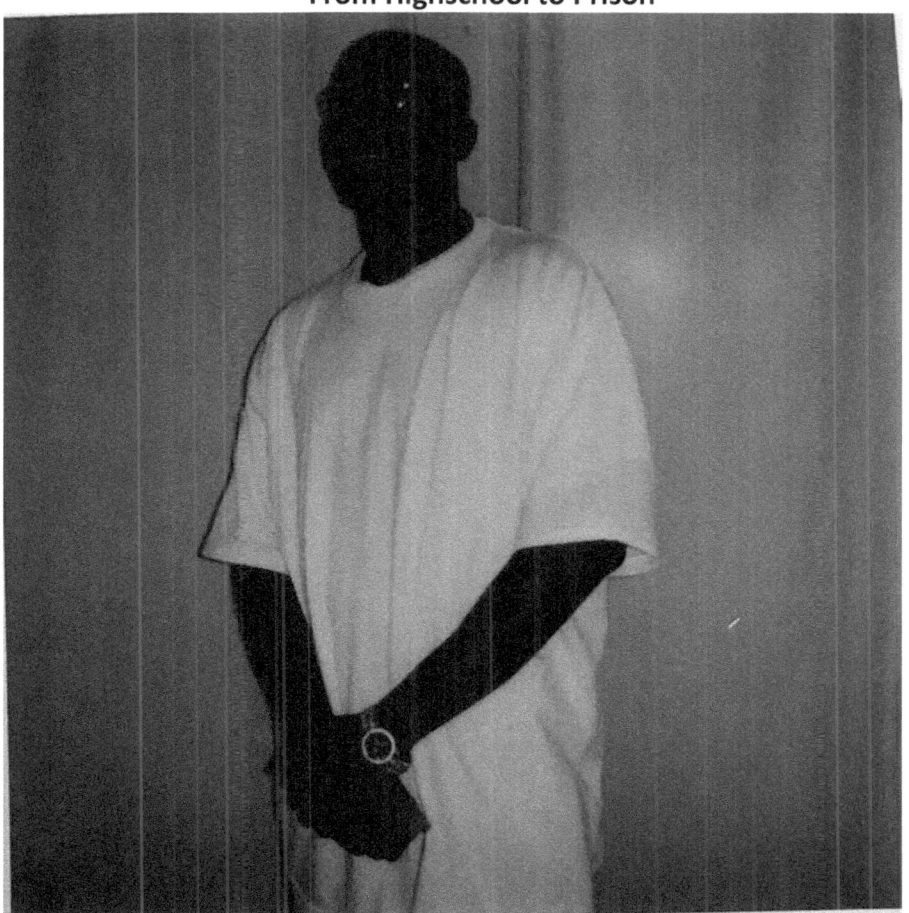

From Highschool to Prison

From Highschool to Prison

From Highschool to Prison

From Highschool to Prison

From Highschool to Prison

From Highschool to Prison

Section II: Being Honest with Myself

From Highschool to Prison

Chapter 5: Time on My Hands

On this prison bus ride from Fayetteville to Butner N.C. all I can do is think back and wonder what if. My freedom was gone within a blank of an eye, now I must listen to CO's and be told when to shower, when to eat, what to wear, when to wake up, when to sleep and so on. When the bus pulled into the prison gates and the officer closed them gates that is when it hit me that I was really in prison and wasn't going to see my son or family for a long time.

As soon as we get off the bus the officers started talking to us like we not even human, they will beat you down if you flex or think about making a move on one of them. When it came time to get dressed out, we all had to take all our clothes off bend over in front of male officers and cough then go wash up and put on some old tight prison uniform and some reject BBC shoes. They then lined us up to go eat in the chow hall, I did not have an appetite after trying to process my thoughts. *I'm really in prison.*

After we left the chow hall, we were assigned our dorms and was given bed sheets, blankets, pillowcase two towels two washcloths, and a few prison uniforms with shorts, socks, and white boxer shorts. I entered my dorm for the first time, found my bunk and laid back and observed what was going on around me. I saw some of everything from different gangs to the gay dudes walking around like women.

I had a chance to use the phone, so I called my mom told them where I was. I had to send them a visitor form to come visit me. I sent everybody visitation forms but never got visits except for one time when my brothers and my cousin came, and they had my son Shaliek with them. That was the day that made my time harder even though I wanted to see them.

Staying Busy

You had to do something when you were in prison. I worked out. I learned about cooking. I took a couple of college classes. Those were the milestones, but the process was even more important. It was just like life. As I reflect on it now, I want anyone who reads to understand that the highlight reels are only valuable on social media. What truly matters is the grind to get where you are going. Each lesson learned, contact made, and decision chosen for your future can be for gain or a loss. From that first day in prison, I was choosing to make the best of the bad. Now, as a free man, I make better every chance I get.

From Highschool to Prison

Work was required if you wanted more than an hour of time outside your cell. I was eventually assigned to work in the kitchen as a dishwasher for .40 cents a day. I could not hold a job when I was in the streets. In prison, my drive to work was enhanced. We cooked in that kitchen for 1500 inmates every day, breakfast, lunch, and dinner.

The most money I could earn was a dollar a day by becoming a cook or a baker. I got promoted to work on the cookline for a dollar a day. I did that for a while knowing that I wanted to be a baker. My moment came quickly, and I moved from the cookline to be a baker. I had to make everything from scratch beside three other guys. I loved the baking department! Cakes, cobbler…everything from scratch. I was making some decent money in the process judging on the inside. We could only spend $40.00 a week no matter how much money your family sent you.

A job in the kitchen meant that we ate better than the other inmates. We always ate before the population. I remember one morning I was eating oatmeal and pork bacon. This guy who works with me sat at my table.

"Do you know what you putting into your body?"

"Food." I said not intending to be flippant. I just did not understand why someone would ask such a question. He then told me his name

"Wisdom." He started sharing things with me about his culture and his way of life. I ended up getting some literature from him and started reading up on all the things he spoke on. I educated myself on the foods

I was consuming, and I ended up letting beef and pork go. I came into the Nation of Gods and Earths and started studying lessons from the father Allah. I respect the lessons and teachings to this day because they really humbled me. They helped me open my eyes to a lot of things.

I became cool with People from different walks of life, from gang members, Christians, Muslims, and of course the 5 Percenters. Working in the kitchen, you get to see everybody represented from the population on the yard. We had to feed them breakfast, lunch, and dinner.

Familiar Faces

I got word from back home that a few dudes I grew up with in SC caught a murder charge in NC. I was thinking I probably would see them at some point. The prison I was incarcerated at is where most people process when around the ages of 19-26. They were around my age.

One day, my expectation was confirmed. I was on the line serving food to the inmates. I saw a familiar face coming down the line to get his tray. It was one of my homeboys from SC, one of those that I heard caught a charge in NC. I hate I had to see him in prison like me, but it felt good to see someone that I knew from back home. We ended up on the same yard. We caught up and talked about what was going on back home. He eventually ended up shipping out to another facility.

From Highschool to Prison

One of my co-defendants ended up to the prison I was at. My homie lance A.K.A Dread was a real dude. I had to pull some strings, but I got him on work detail in the kitchen with me. He was already a baker at the prison he came from, so that helped me get him in the kitchen even faster. We were together every day on the yard, in the dorm, and working in the kitchen. After a while, we had the kitchen on lock. All the officers respected us. We could bake whatever we wanted and eat whatever we wanted. We had officers bringing us food from the outside and everything.

The First Loss Inside

I was paged to come to the chaplain's office one day. The chaplain gave me the phone and told me I needed to call home. I didn't know what was going on, I called home to find out my grandfather had passed away. I was devastated. The sense that I was inside came rushing back after having been captivated with my progress. It was progress. But it was progress on the inside. I was not free.

I couldn't attend the funeral because they only allowed bereavement travel if the deceased was immediate family. The supervisor in the kitchen let me take the rest of the day off. I just went back to my cell and cried. Being locked up and losing a loved one is a hurtful feeling. Knowing you will never see them again and you can't see them for that last time, is devastating. All you can do is think back to the last time you saw them and rest on the memories you made before you went inside. I had to pull myself together with the promise that I would not be inside forever.

A few weeks went by, and I got papers served to me saying I must go back to court on other charges in Richmond County. When that day came, I had to be shackled down and transported by an officer from the prison to the Richmond County jail. It felt good to be outside of prison riding on the highway seeing people living and going about their days without a care in the world. On the other hand, it didn't feel good not knowing if I was about to add more time to my sentence. My court date was on February 14th, Valentine's day.

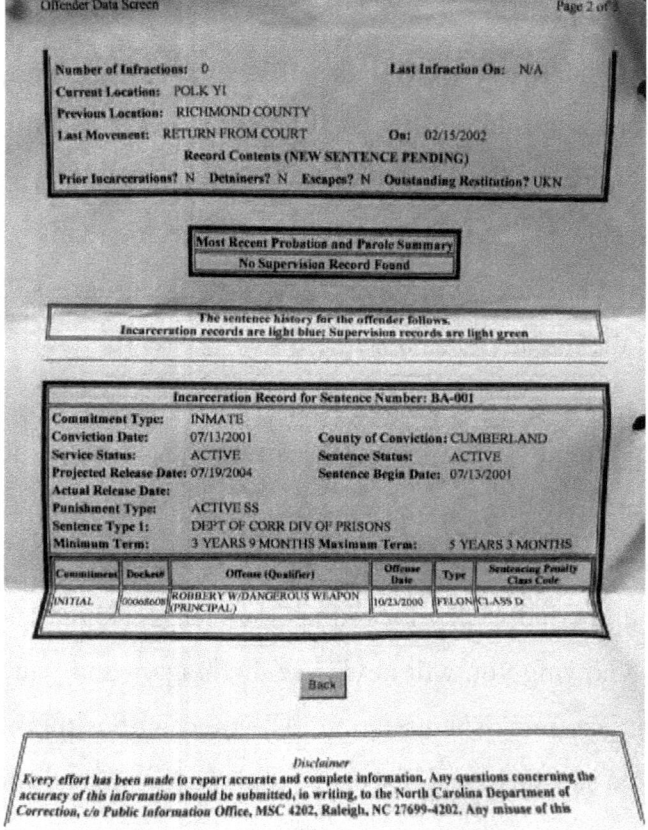

From Highschool to Prison

I was hit with four more years on top of the four years I was already doing. I just knew I was going home in 2004. I set my mind and my calendar to endure until that date. The judge gave me more time extending my stay through 2008. I was sucker punched in the gut. The wind leaped from my lungs as the time calculation stood like a bully before me. When I returned to the prison, I floated deflated to my cell and laid down looking up at the ceiling. I thought about how matter of fact the judge acted as hit me with more time. I wanted to be home by my son's first year in school. That was no longer a viable plan. I had to call home and break the news to my family. I had to inform them that I received more time. I had to adjust to the reality that I would not be home until 2008.

Home Going Service
In Loving Memory
Of
Deacon Warren Adams

Sunrise
August 25, 1923

Sunset
September 23, 2001

Saturday, September 29, 2001
3:00 P.M.

Berea Convention Center
Bennettsville, South Carolina

Reverend Fest Bethea, Officiating

Chapter 6: More Work to Do

Reading more and Traveling beyond my environment, I learned that there were more ways to get money beyond the illegal. We would ride a job to Raleigh to a college to paint, move furniture, or something else. I was making $21 per week.

I was single minded and focused. I had to keep a clear head and stay on point, so I started reading more books and educating myself. I also took college courses that the prison offered to us from a nearby community college. I studied books on real estate, business, and the music industry. A lot of the guys used to tell me that I would be a millionaire one day because they saw how focused I was.

The more I tried to block out what was happening in the real world, the more stories of tragedy came at me. I was receiving letters from people back home about how this person got shot or that person was killed. As time passed, I started losing family members. One of my grandfathers passed away a year before I went to prison, but the rest of my grandparents passed away while I was in prison. I never had a chance to say goodbye or nothing. I just had to sit in prison and take it.

The Quest

When I learned that I could be eligible for work release my last three years in prison, I did everything in my power to stay out of trouble. This one day my temper got the best of me. I was in my cell resting one day before I was scheduled to work in the kitchen. Someone was outside tapping the window with a rock. When I look up to see who was playing at my cell window the rock was thrown hard and crack the window, so I punched the window out and started blanking. The CO's came and put me in the hole.

I stayed in the hole for 28 days behind that, but I had to use my head to get out of there and not get charged for punching out the window. I happen to see one of the lieutenants pass the hole I was in. I stopped him. He was surprised to see me in the hole because I use to hook him up with all kinds of food from the kitchen. I told him what happened, and he told me he will get me out with no charge. He did just that.

Sad to say but after them 28 days in the hole I felt like a free man. I was able to walk on the yard, lift weights, play ball, it just felt good to be out the hole. When you walk out of there you feel free, but you are still in prison. I finally got my job back in the kitchen with the

From Highschool to Prison

renewed goal to stay out of trouble so I can get sent to a work release prison.

For some reason, this guy I worked with in the kitchen kept trying me. It got to the point where I had to confront him. I told him, "When we leave the kitchen and get back to our dorm, scrap up." He had a few days left before he was to be released from prison. We got back to the dorm and everybody went outside to the yard for recreation except me, him, my partner Felipe, and one of his partners. We went into a room and my homie looked out for me while I beat the breaks off this dude. After that, I got nothing but respect from him. He ended up going home with the black eye I gave him.

My Review

A few months went by, and my caseworker called me in for my review. She told me I was going to be transferred to Wake Advance in Raleigh, a green clothes prison where we were not under the gun. I wasn't eligible for work release yet, but I wasn't far from it.

When I got to Wake prison, I saw a few guys I knew from Polk that I use to work with in the kitchen. They told me how sweet the prison was and how much better it was than Polk. I ran into a few five percenters and started building with them every day. We had a lot of respect on the yard, nobody tried us. One brother by the name of Shyallah, became my right-hand man.

My caseworker assigned me to this job that allows us to leave prison and go do work in different parts of North Carolina. I had it made on this job. We got paid $21.00 a week and we got to go outside of the prison and see real people. We could talk to people as well. The only difference between us was that we were in prison uniforms and they weren't.

My co-defendant Lance got transferred to the same prison I was at. He ended up on the same work crew with me. The guy we worked for was cool. He used to take some of the guys to meet their wives and their family members. Some of them would go home and have sex with their wives. We would come back to pick them up after a day of work. While they were doing all that, I was buying whole cartons of Newports and sneaking them back into the prison. I sold one single for a dollar each. I was more concerned with getting money, and I was amassing revenue.

On one occasion, we had to do a job at this college near rocky mount and this girl was checking me out. I had her to meet me in the men's bathroom and gave her the business. I didn't know her name. She didn't know me. She just knew I was in prison. I told my boy Lance about it, and he got right the next day.

Time was starting to go by faster because I was doing more. Things really got better when my homie Shy started kicking it with my caseworker. She was cool. She made sure we had whatever we wanted.

From Highschool to Prison

I didn't have to sneak cigarettes into the prison no more. She would bring them for us. We had cell phones, mp3 players, you name it. We ate good every day. She called me into her office one day and told me that the governor of North Carolina wanted me to come work for him at the governor's mansion. I thought it over. If I took the mansion job, I couldn't get work release. The mansion job didn't pay the inmates much, but it goes a long way on your resume once you get out of prison. I ended up turning the job down because I knew if I received work release, I could come home straight away.

Work Release Transfer

A few months went by and I was finally eligible for work release. But a waiting list was my obstacle at that point. I had to rise to the top of the list before I would be transferred to a work release prison. I put in my request to my caseworker to be transferred to Monroe NC. Like always, she made it happen for me.

Before I got transferred to Monroe, my uncle Johnny came to visit me. Johnny is my dad's twin brother. He lived in Raleigh. It was good to see him. The memory is imprinted because I hadn't seen him in years, and I hadn't had a visitor in years.

I arrived at the work release prison in Monroe, a small prison that held maybe 200 people. Ninety-five percent of them were on work release at real jobs getting real money. I had to wait until a job came open before I could go to work. When it did come open, I didn't want it, but I took it anyway just to get off the prison camp for a few hours each day. The job was called paving and grading. I had to help put hot tar on the roads and pave driveways out in the hot sun. I knew I couldn't do this job for long. I ended up talking to a few guys at the prison to help me get on at this company called M&L Riggers. I put in a request to my case manager to switch jobs, and I got the job. My time was downhill from this point. My boss was cool. He used to take us out to eat, to the mall, and more.

Street clothes were allowed at this prison as long as we were off the prison camp grounds. We had to return to our prison clothes when we got back onto the prison grounds. I had my brothers to send me clothes and shoes.

I was making good money for a person in prison. All the money I was making was going into a savings account in Raleigh NC that the prison set up for work release inmates. We were only allowed to spend $40.00 a week no matter how much money we had in the account. They gave us cards that we could use only in prison to purchase items. Every Monday another $40.00 would credit to the card. We weren't allowed to have cash, but of course I did. I asked my boss man to take me to the mall one day to buy my son some Jordans. I had someone I knew to mail them to him for me.

My account in Raleigh was stacking up. they gave us statements every week so we could track how much money was in our account and how much we spent. When holidays came around, they let us send money home out of our account. I used to send money to my family to make sure my son had a good Christmas. I also did what I could for my nephews.

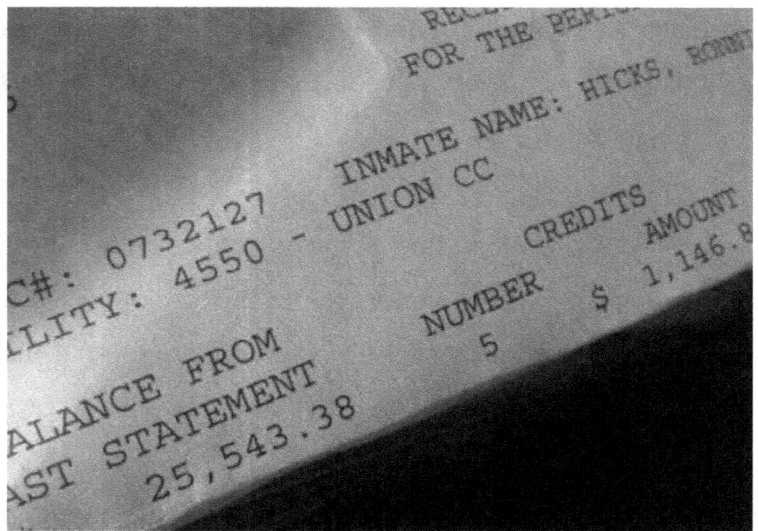

Visitation was on the weekends. Even though I was closer to home, I still wasn't getting visitors like I thought I would. Rather than let that get me down, I became the camera man on the weekends. I took pictures of all the inmates and their family members during visitation hours. I met a lot of people each day. The additional perk was seeing a lot of pretty woman on visitation day. This one girl I met when I was at the prison in Raleigh came to Monroe to visit me for the first time. She was beautiful. I just knew she was going to be my lady when I got out.

From Highschool to Prison

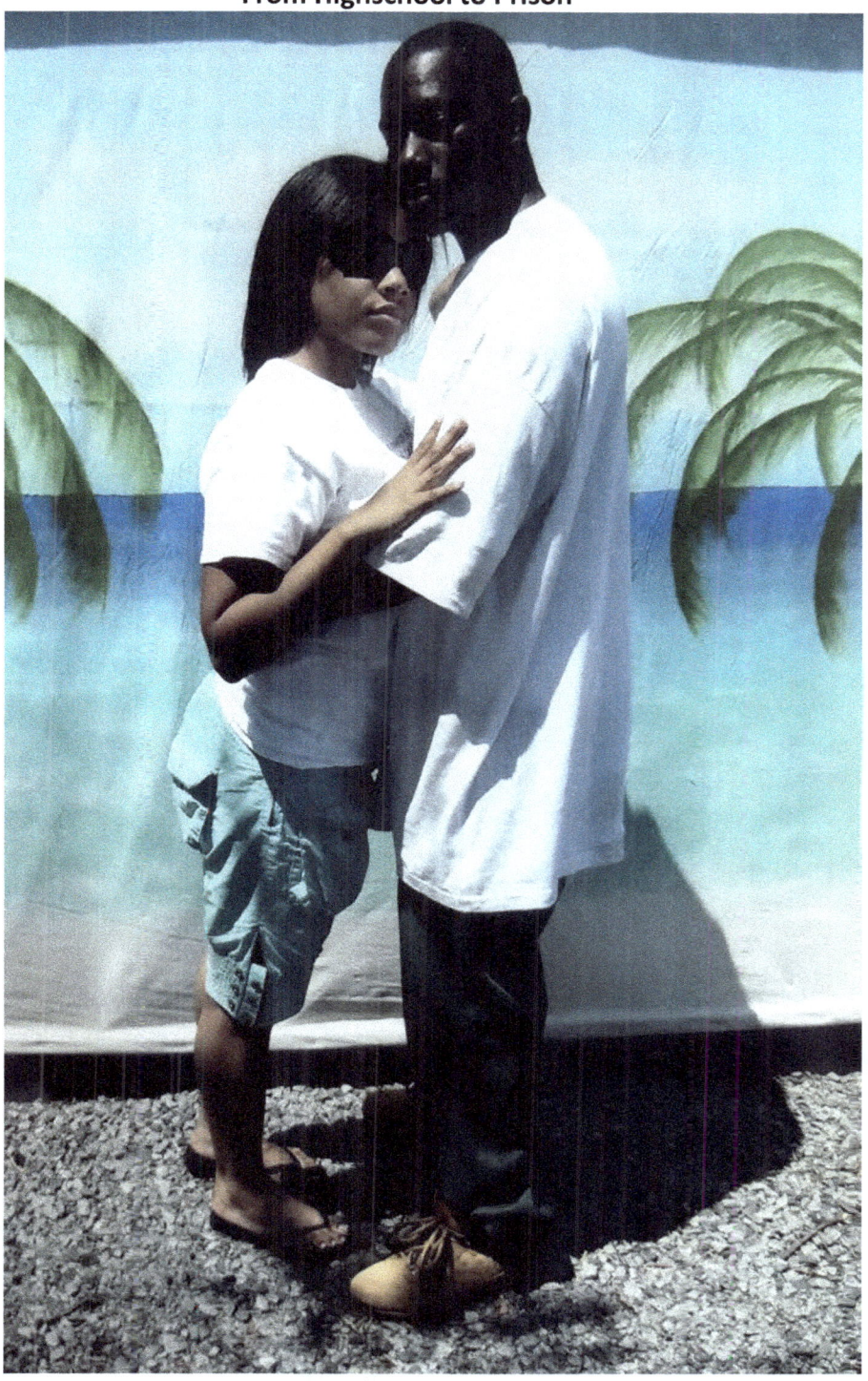

From Highschool to Prison

My brother G Money came to see me one weekend. It was good to see him I had not seen him in years. He caught me up on what was going on with him and his family, and we took a few pictures before he left.

After visitation, most of us will go workout or shoot ball. Working out was an everyday thing for me unless we got off work late, after the yard was closed. I remember when I first got to prison, I couldn't lift 90 pounds. I was now working out with 245 pounds. My max was 315 pounds on the bench press. Working out was a way for me to pass time, I would put my headphones in and block out everything. I used to find myself thinking about my hood, my family, friends, and girls I had dealings with. I would also think about my son of course. I used to wonder what their life was like now, and what they were doing with themselves.

My subscription to my hometown newspaper the Marlboro Herald allowed me to see people I knew. They looked different. They were grown now. Some of them were doing well. A lot of them were doing badly. Every week, I was reading about people I knew going to jail. One week I got the newspaper, and my son was featured. I didn't have that many pictures of him, so when I saw him on that float in the Clio parade with a crown on his head, it made my day.

From Highschool to Prison

From Highschool to Prison

From Highschool to Prison

Homegoing Services for

Mrs. Queen Esther Adams

Saturday, October 20, 2007
11:00 am

St. Beulah
Missionary Baptist Church
Bennettsville, SC

Reverend Fest Bethea,
Pastor

October 24, 1930

October 14, 2007

My yearning desire is to depart and be with Christ, for that is far, far better.
Philippians 1:23

Chapter 7: Reading and Learning and Growing

Think and Grow Rich, Rich Dad Poor Dad, and other books were my introduction to another life. I learned from multiple books I poured over. I gained knowledge in the How Tos of business, real estate, and trucking. I learned the 5 Percenter's Lessons and other perspectives to add to my practical knowledge. I studied about starting a record label. I amassed contact lists for all the major labels, newspapers, and magazines. I subscribed to my hometown newspaper when I had the chance and received that.

The 5 Percenters have lessons they call Mathematics. They request that you study, learn, and recite the constructs to advance in the levels. I advanced with ease finding that I had a knack for learning I had never tapped into before. Learning about different ways of life provided a solid preparation for my return home. I knew how to set up a business from nothing. I learned how to register an LLC, request and EIN number, and other processes for launching. I took a ton of notes in the margins of books. I used them as reference texts for each venture that I wanted to start.

THE WORST THING THAT EVER HAPPENED TO ME IS THE BEST THING THAT HAPPEN TO ME.

The first step was to learn and know myself. That is the priority in business. You must know what you like to eat before you can put together a meal. You must take care of yourself before you can take care of others. My advice to other would-be entrepreneurs: Be truthful and honest. Refuse to lie to yourself. Lies will always come back to bite you. If you are unable to produce something, don't say you can do it. Represent only what you can do. Honesty creates a relationship of integrity.

More to Life

You think that the way you grew up is the way of life. There is more than your neighborhood and your block. There are more opportunities out in the world. My experience and learning in prison opened my eyes. I was on parole for 9 months after I was released. I walked on eggshells not wanting to return to prison. I could not go back to South Carolina or risk violation of my parole. That situation meant that I was not able to get back into the same environment. I learned what I learned, but I do not believe I could have maintained if I had moved back to South Carolina. The police had changed, new snitches, a new game. The circles you moved within 8 years prior are not the safe places they were before you were locked up.

I have seen people jump from third tier of the prison block, shanked, beaten with locks in socks and more. I remember once I was serving chow in the line. I watched an inmate sneaking up on another inmate. He began beating him mercilessly. Sometimes it was a lock. Sometimes it was soap. The lesson was to continue to be alert.

I applied that to my life after prison. I had to watch my back and guard against a violation of parole. The environment, the quick money, and the desire for things creeps up on you. But I learned to stay alert and make sure I move toward my goals without distractions.

Some people go into the prison system and don't come out. I lost my grandparents while I was locked up. I lost time with my son because I was incarcerated. I can't remember the last time I was around them or the last conversation we had. I missed so much. I could not reclaim any of that experience.

It is not just you going to prison. The people who care about you miss out as well. If they do visit you, they must travel out to the country to see you. I was in a whole different state. I say that South Carolina made me, but North Carolina paid me.

From Highschool to Prison

I used to stash cash in items I bought from the canteen. No matter how much money you have, you cannot spend more than $40 per week. You cannot use cash legally while in prison, but you can use cash for various needs. If I was able to get my hands on cash, I stashed it. I got cash by making moves. The commerce inside was expansive. Over my time, I sold cigarettes, performed favors like phone calls, and other small things most of which I cannot remember. I stashed in creative spots to avoid the violation of contraband.

Coming Home to Karma

When I came home, I did not have it in me to sell drugs. I had been gone too long. I also had business mindset within me. I made real money in the last 3 years of my sentence. I saved $25,000 when I was in prison. I was paroled in NC and began to build right there adjacent to my home state of South Carolina.

Dec 2008, I was paroled. My first business was a boutique. I was still working in the chicken plant that was my work program while awaiting parole. I promoted shows while working at the chicken plant. I was also working at another plant. I sold shoes through my boutique.

I was a trusting businessman willing to go the extra mile for my customers. A girl asked me to deliver some shoes for her. It was not an unusual request. A ready customer was always preferrable to sitting idle in the storefront or on a corner.

I arrived at the location we set up to meet and was slightly unnerved when she made an excuse for me to pull around the rear of the building. My laptop and merchandise were comfortably in the back seat. I turned the car off with the keys in the ignition and invited her to the backseat to view the shoe selection. I stood just outside the car discussing the value of the brands represented.

As I'm showing her the goods, a guy put a gun to my leg. He ran through my pockets. He didn't now that I'm fresh out of prison. Just about a year had passed. I did not have the will to sell drugs and certainly was not robbing, but I was still a fighter. He looked over the top of the car checking for witnesses. I took the opportunity of his split focus to grab the gun, a .38 as I remember it. I attempted to get the gun out of his hands. He started screaming like I was robbing him. We fell while struggling with the gun. I went for the gun. He sprinted for the car. I got up as we were both disoriented and ran to safety. He jumped in my car, started it, and drove off. The police got involved because I had to report my car stolen, but I ended up handling everything on my own and found my car after a week. Karma is real. This was what I was doing that got me locked up. I robbed a guy at gun point.

Fly straight and create the karma that you want. I could not be mad about being mugged. It was destined to come back on me. I knew how it felt for the person I wronged. My goal now is to invest the type of karma that will yield the best for me and my family.

From Highschool to Prison

I stand up in the community. I lead by example. Be someone who promotes the positives in your community. It is so easy to be negative. I was that person that found my way into the negatives, but I am even more motivated to promote the positives in my community.

I remember taking a van and two cars full of children from South Carolina to Charlotte for my son's 10th birthday. This is something that the children who attended will never forget. I am about to visit McDonald's in my hometown after the push of the latest stimulus dies down. I will set an amount to spend and treat families to dinner. I reach out on Facebook periodically and do CashApp promotions paying for dinner. Families only must verify the number of kids in their family, and I send them $10 per child. This is just a sample of how I determined to give back to the world. It does not always have to be monetary, but giving back is what I do. It is the same approach that I use to invest in business ventures.

From Highschool to Prison

PCAR180A (80)

NORTH CAROLINA
POST-RELEASE SUPERVISION CERTIFICATE

IN ACCORDANCE WITH THE PROVISIONS OF SECTION 15A-1368.2 OF THE GENERAL STATUTES OF NORTH CAROLINA, RONNIE HICKS HAS BEEN RELEASED FROM THE NORTH CAROLINA DEPARTMENT OF CORRECTION ON POST-RELEASE SUPERVISION.

RONNIE HICKS WILL BE SUBJECTED TO THE CONDITIONS OF POST-RELEASE SUPERVISION AS ESTABLISHED BY THE NORTH CAROLINA POST-RELEASE SUPERVISION AND PAROLE COMMISSION.

THE POST-RELEASE SUPERVISEE'S COUNTY OF SUPERVISION WILL BE UNION.

UNDER THE PROVISION OF SECTIONS 15A-1368.3 AND 15A-1368.6 A POST-RELEASE SUPERVISEE MAY BE RETURNED TO PRISON UP TO THE REMAINING ON THE MAXIMUM IMPOSED TERM, IF THE SUPERVISEE VIOLATES A CONDITION OF SUPERVISION IMPOSED BY THE NORTH CAROLINA POST-RELEASE SUPERVISION AND PAROLE COMMISSION.

THEODIS BECK
SECRETARY, NORTH CAROLINA
DEPARTMENT OF CORRECTION

THIS THE 1ST DAY OF DECEMBER 2008

Chapter 8: Trust Issues

My First Born

When I engaged my first child's mother, we were not in a relationship. I liked her but did not want to be in a relationship. My homeboy introduced me to her. He was messing with her cousin. It was a, "She got a cousin" situation. She got my name on her fingernails and told everyone that I paid for it. It was a ploy to let all the girls know that I was hers.

She came up pregnant and I was down with taking care of the responsibility. But I was still out in the streets. I was only there for one Christmas before I was locked up. We did not talk while I was in prison. I wrote my son from lockup. My brothers made sure he was okay as much as they could. I was in the county jail for nine months. I appreciated the family support and them being there in the flesh where I could not.

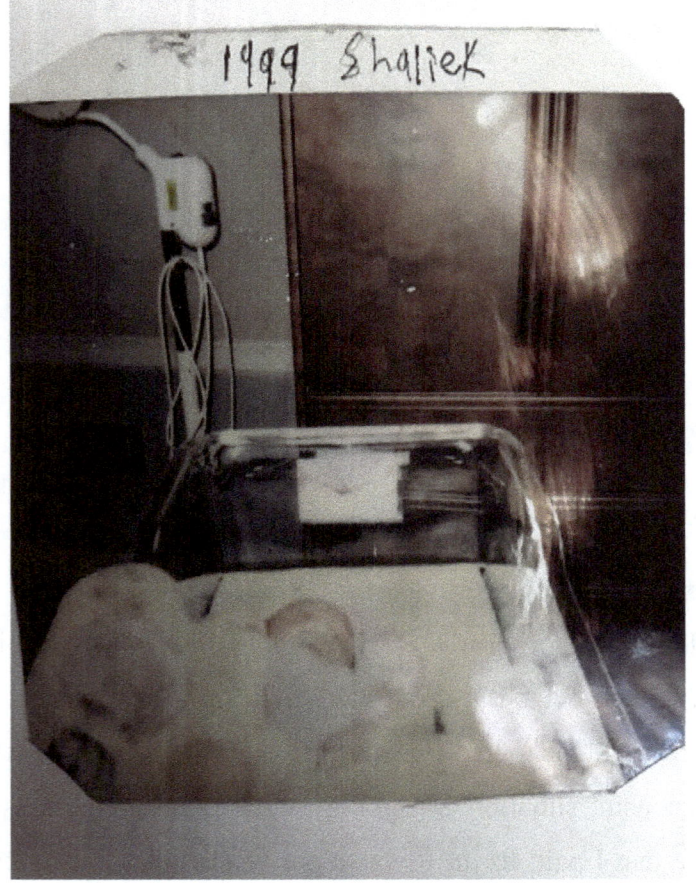

I grew up with my dad and mom in the household. So family is important to me. I was not there for my oldest while incarcerated, but I love children. I love my son. I brought him out to live with me when I got out of prison. I made sure he did not do what I did when I was his age. I took him out of the hood and showed him a different life. He saw me open businesses. He saw me work every day.

From Highschool to Prison

My Highschool Sweetheart

I had a girlfriend in high school that taught me about loss more than any other experience. I always made sure my lady was laced up. We had a great bond. We had a bond that was seemingly unbreakable. Her sister told me one day that she was throwing up. She had a baby. She knew the signs. We talked about my excitement about having my second child. She was in church and her parents did not want the embarrassment of a 16-year-old teen mother. Her parents forced her to abort our child.

After the abortion, our relationship was strained but still connected. We were still cool. I had other interests that I pursued, but I would always return to her. In fact, I was supposed to go and see her the day I got locked up. She tried to visit me while I was incarcerated in the county jail. I saw her from the window. She could not get in. She was the one who held me down while I was locked up. She wrote me every week. All those girls who liked me and none of them cared when I was locked up. My relationship with her allowed me to see what I wanted in a woman. Most women were impressed by what I had and what I could give them. She was solid because of who I was.

She was my connection to the neighborhood. The news was comforting. She wrote me once to let me know that she was diagnosed with cancer. She would send me pictures of her treatment and the aftermath. She fought it and beat it.

As time goes on, the letter frequency decreased. I appreciated the time that she did give me. I put myself in that situation. I could not expect her to put her life on hold just because my life was limited. After the letters stopped, we did not talk except for on Facebook. We have never connected in person again.

You will lose not being present. I see many men who want their cake and eat it too. They see women as conquests and exploratory experiences. If you have your main, the bond is not just about cake. It is about more. You cannot put a price on loyalty. Ride or die is more than a notion. It sounds good, but when it is time to put it to the test, people are nowhere to be found. The ones that you mistreat are the ones that hold you down. If you have mistreated them, you feel bad. If I had one regret, it would be that I did not always recognize how to step into the manhood I understand now.

From Highschool to Prison
Making A Life

I met my second child's mother while on work release at a chicken plant. She was going to college to be a nurse but dropped out for personal reasons. She began working at the plant. I remember seeing her and being attracted. I would talk to her in the locker room. I let her know that I was soon to be released. I was forward telling her that I would like to get to know her. She giggled and said OK.

She was the one who took me to the bank with my $25,000. I had already paid for an apartment. She was with me when I purchased the air mattress and some essentials. She spent the night a few nights. She trained me about texting, MySpace, and the current technology. I got my new driver's license with her car. She was living with her parents, but I told her I wanted her to move in. She held my hand when I got out of prison. I stayed in that apartment for 3 years.

GEORGETOWNE MANOR APARTMENTS
MADRID APARTMENTS
CIRCLE DIRVE APARTMENTS
BURKE VILLAGE APARTMENTS

TO: NEW RESIDENTS

RE: ELECTRICITY

Electricity must be put into your name before you will be allowed to move in. This can be handled with the power company by going to their office, filling out an application, giving them your move-in date and paying a deposit. You must bring this form filled out by the power company before we can give you the key.

The power company is the City of Monroe.

Thank you.

Resident RONNIE HICKS Power Co. _____

Apt # 1217 E. SUNSET DR #5 By _____

Date 12-8-08 Date _____

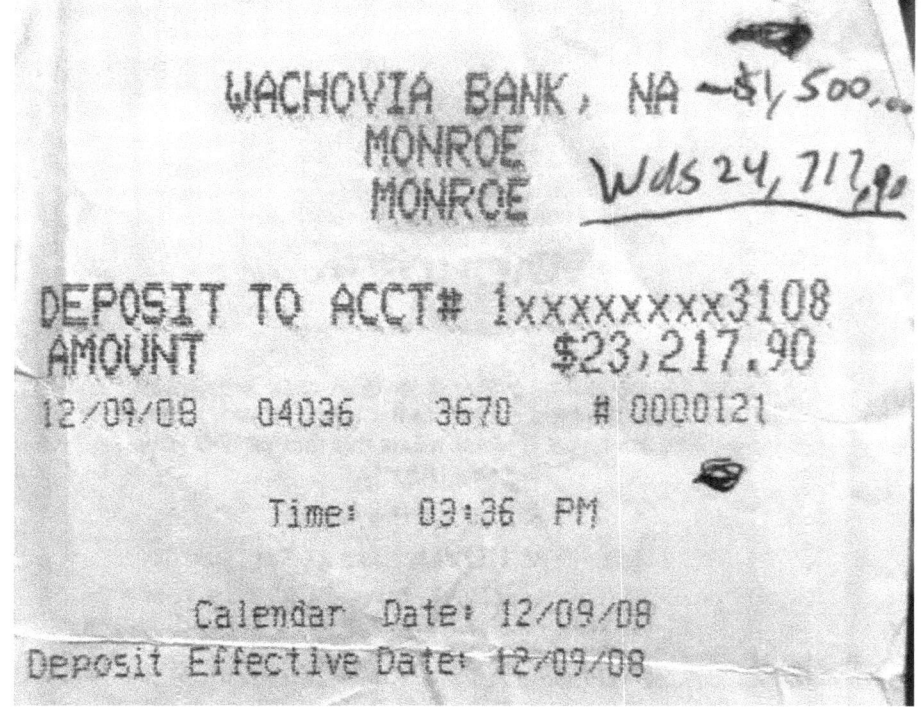

She was into cosmetology. She was doing hair prior to meeting me. I noticed her skills and offered to set her up back in her hometown where she had clientele. I opened her a hair salon. I put in the work to find her a location and schedule a ribbon cutting with the chamber of commerce. It was a 35-minute drive but one she was used to visiting her mom periodically.

I got a house by the time I was 29. She had trust issues. It started while we were in the chicken plant. I was giving too much conversation with females at the plant. I was popular. I was promoting shows. I was out attending to relationships in ways that I felt were innocent. She never caught me in anything unseemly, but she was not comfortable with her being in the shop and me being at the chicken plant.

From Highschool to Prison

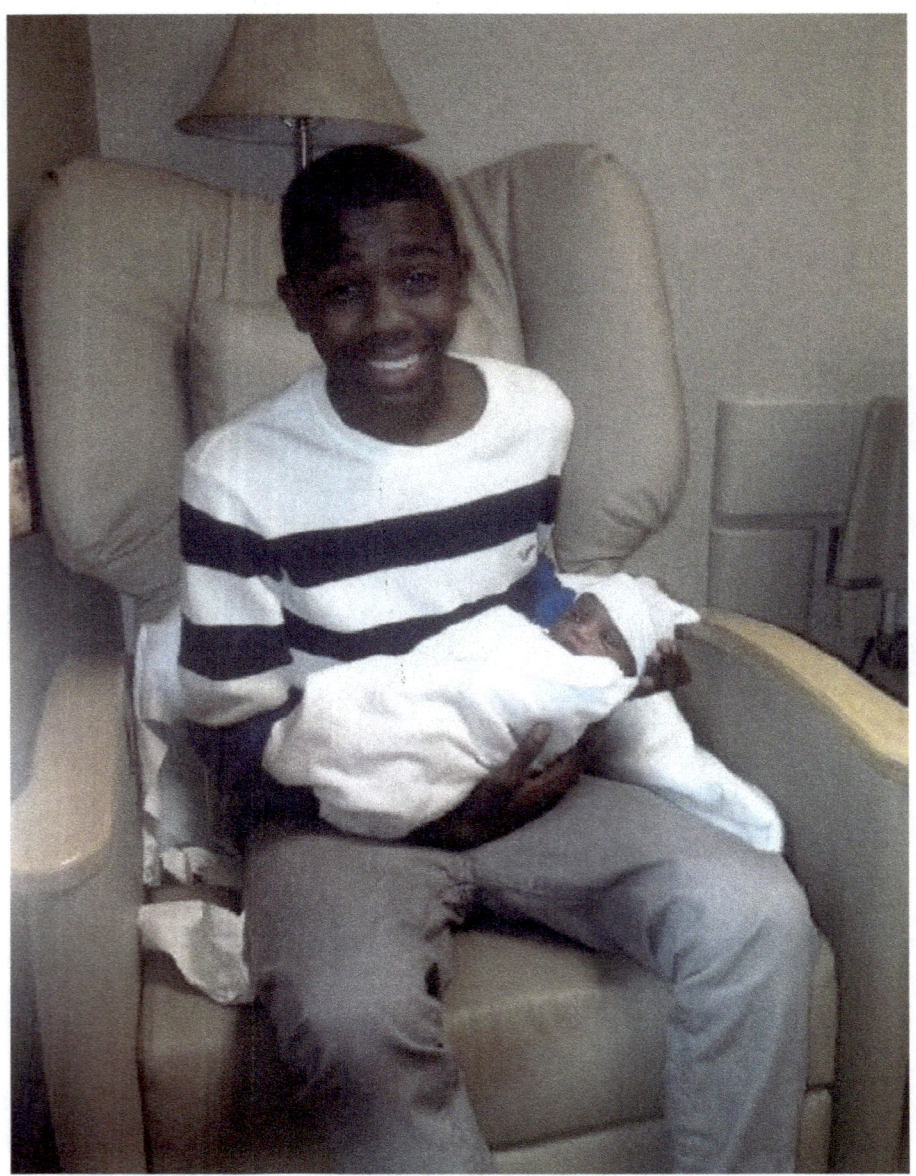

I remember I had a party back in my hometown for my birthday. I had a lot of people waiting on me. She called just before I left that night. She informed me that she did not want a relationship anymore. She wanted to move back with her mother and take my son. My first thought was that she had found someone else. She told me that she wanted to focus on raising our son alone. I ended up having to engage the court to see my son.

I do not want to say that it made me cold, but I learned that investments are never appreciated in the way that you expect when you deal with human beings. No matter how well you believe you treat a person, their experience is what matters. I never thought I would face a situation where a woman I wanted to be with and raise my son with would choose to leave me. It opened my eyes.

My brother and I were talking about the lessons the other day. You must know who you are putting your time and energy into. I knew I needed someone to hold my hand when I got out of prison. I did not know anything about the world I was entering. But I knew about business and the grind. I may have put more, too much, of my focus into the pursuit of happiness while others were content with their station in life.

I tell my sons to this day: You must choose your mate wisely. That is not just your wife but any woman that you connect with. Pull up in something less than what you deserve or can afford. Check to see whether a woman is interested in material things or whether she is about more substance. You want a woman that will hold you down if you are living under a bridge. That is a woman you can build a mansion with.

My Love Story

Around August that year, a pool party was popping in Florence. After the party, I ran into a short, redbone. I brought her back to my hometown for a football game. No one knew who she was. I was showing her off like a trophy. She was in her last year of school. As I was getting to know her, we had not messed around.

I had pictures of her when I got locked up. I was in SC at the mall and saw her working as a manager in a store. I had my oldest son with me. "You don't know who I am?" She did not recognize me. This was 10 years later. She wanted to kick it with me. I had a talent show in her town in the works and she came out with her children to see. I had a son on the way. She fell back after that.

After my son's mother left me telling me that she wanted to focus solely on raising our son. I moved the girl from SC to NC with me. She transferred to a clothing store in NC. She and her kids now live with me. She gave birth to my only little girl.

When I got locked up, she was still calling my home. I explained that I was locked up through a call on 3-way. There was no conversation after that. I had not known her like that. I could not blame her and did not know when I was getting out.

From Highschool to Prison

I ran into her without any preplan. I had her picture on my mirror while I was in prison. I never thought I would be with her. I was not looking for her. I only held the picture to remind me of the life I left.

We talk about it periodically. It is crazy because we lived our lives separately. I faded from her memory as she made the choices to live her life. It was not a full month after we met, and I was gone. She does not remember the time before, but we connected in the present.

The connection we had was natural. That connection is what we share today after sitting down with the maturity beyond our youth. We share the business mindset and our managerial hustle. We are similar in that. We share that grind. And that is my lesson. I have learned to connect with natural connections, prioritize loyalty, and build a foundation for my children.

Section III: Investment

Chapter 9: Investment in Self

Creating work ethic through failures. The example of life creates the drive to build and grow.

Find Yourself First

I also engaged men who had been there for multiple years. They were sharp. I soaked up their information with eagerness. I was exposed to people who were enmeshed with the Nation of Islam. I took elements from the 5 percenters, Christians, and Muslims. Groups formed in the yard like a bazaar of information. I found myself moving from group to group enjoying the learning. That was the beginning of ordering books and teaching myself.

I got into dozens of books and read about different cultures, religions, and ways of life. I found my interest in entrepreneurship and music. I read voraciously to feed those interests. I established a work

From Highschool to Prison

ethic extending that sense of hustle that I learned as a child. The drive to work came from the simple choices of the prison. You either work or go into the hole. I chose to work. Outside prison, the choices are more complex, but simple in when you know who you are and your interests.

It is hard to explain to you how to find yourself beyond reviewing options. Hustle was always within me, I just had to direct it toward my advantage. It does not matter whether you went to prison or not. The difference between progress and stagnation is the decision you make to be the best in your situation, learn, and advance. I chose to switch it up. People I left were still doing the same thing when I came back. They had not made the choice to switch up. I came home loaning money and helping people.

You must change your perspective no matter what environment you are in. Find the people, places, and things that go with what you want for your life. For example, if you barely made it out of high school partying and playing video games, you will need to change something when you go to college. You cannot talk the same and make the same choices when you are attempting to make certain moves. You cannot move in leveled up circles wearing the same clothes you wore on the block. Growth is what it takes.

Many people say that they are in a struggle situation because they are a product of their environment. But that is a cop out. You just don't want to do better. You are taking the easy route. You would rather be comfortable than challenging yourself into something new. Some suggest that you turn it off and on. They counsel you to keep your hood knowledge while adding the ability to operate in a corporate environment. I say don't put yourself in the situations that are struggle situations. You may be able to fight and hold your own in struggle situations, but don't put yourself out where you are unsafe and risking your progress. You may get out there on a limb and lose everything because the hood is comfortable.

Don't worry about what people say who are not where you are or have not experienced what you want to be. Don't be a follower. Break the generational curse. Seek more information and challenge yourself to live in those environments that are less comfortable. Realize that they are only uncomfortable for a time. You will adjust to the new normal.

Relationships

Establish who you are so that your significant other can determine if they want to be with the person you are. Confidence is the primary achievement. People can tell whether you are a good fit for them right away. If you are attempting to deceive people into connecting, you set up a situation where you will burn bridges eventually. Slick, sneaky, and conniving will get you in the end. It may seem that you are getting somewhere in the beginning, but the farther you get, the harder the fall.

From Highschool to Prison

Your mindset is the beginning of the change. The confidence results from your authenticity and your choices to do right by people. As you see the outcomes and the sustainability, you are more encouraged. You will engage people with good intentions and find positive relationships result.

For example, you may be tempted to engage with a person of the opposite sex because of what they can do for you. You may have learned that behavior from the streets. If you never changed those habits, you will continue the negative behavior. It may not be intentional, but you need to be more intentional with your choices and how you engage with others. You must first admit that you are using them. Be honest with yourself. Realize what the experience should be like. Relationships must be about reciprocity—give and take on both sides. Intentionality means that you make sure you are an asset not a liability. Even if you are not working a job, you must show appreciation through your job search, helping around the house, and providing healthy attention.

I have seen a lot of guys that meet women when they are in prison The women are good until the dude gets out and begins to deal with them. I suggest that guys get themselves together before they engage with women. Ensure that you can support her holistically and not diminish or bring her down.

Mind and Body

The connection between mind, body, and behavior is well documented. I also see the results in my family. My father died a few days before I graduated high school. He was only 49 years old. He would drink and get pissy drunk. His weight fluctuated widely. He was often in diabetic comas.

When I went to prison, I learned about the toxins I was putting into my body. I never touched alcohol and other drugs, but the meats and processed foods that I was comfortable consuming. I changed my lifestyle and diet. I began to work out with vigor. I stopped eating pork and beef.

I came home and did not maintain the workout routine. I am getting back to that. Now I don't eat any meat at all. You can make those choices in your life more easily after you research the issues of disease, benefits of exercise, and options in your diet. I found out about the process of cancers and the different options surrounding meat. I used to eat turkey and chicken every day. I cut back gradually. I cut out meat in one meal per day and changed the habits of what I ordered when I went out.

Another important action is to surround yourself with people who are on the same track as you. If you surround yourself with people who steal, you will be a thief. If you surround yourself with 5 millionaires, you will soon be the sixth. Spend time with people who eat healthily and exercise regularly. The healthy routine will not be foreign or abnormal. They will also share experiences and knowledge that encourages healthy choices and a healthy lifestyle.

Chapter 10: Investment in Your Business

Being an entrepreneur is not for everyone, but hustling is not just a skill of the streets. You can work a 9 to 5 and apply those hustling skills to your advantage. Many people, including those that come out of prison, do not know that they can have a job and a business even with a felony. Do not settle and accept what is given to you.

I worked at the chicken plant. I operated a business as well. I had a hair salon. They didn't want me to run a business. They wanted me to work a job. I worked at several other jobs as well as promoting celebrities. I never had a hard time getting work. I met a ton of great people. A year after your release, you can train for the CDL in a trucking course. You need a truck to test with. You can access those through personal connections and employment connections.

The system is happy to put you back in if you violate parole. Options are vital to ensure that you do not go back. So many get paroled and return to the lives that put them in prison in the first place. Establish openness to the change of your life. Get involved in information like motivational videos, reading inspirational books, and discovering what you enjoy in life. It can be construction, needlepoint, or painting, but you need to identify it. The brain is a muscle that you must train. Feed it with positivity and you will exhibit positivity on the outside.

Time must be invested wisely. In prison, you are not free to do what you want, but you do have time in your mind. Your mind will develop and train toward what you put into it. The good thing about prison is that you do not have the distractions of the outside world. Appointments, hanging out, women, and more are not available. You can learn whatever you want to learn. I took advantage of the time and learned. I created a university in my mind and fed it with information. It makes the time go faster, but more importantly; it creates a foundation for sustainable choices as you prepare to go home.

If you prepare yourself with a mindset toward learning, growth, development, you are ready when you gain release. I was convinced that the investment of time called prison was going to yield a return for me.

Creating Reality
The girl I met at the chicken plant was good at doing hair. She would do hair in our apartment. She was not thinking about opening in a building. I was. I was always about business. I applied the same hype

that I would later apply to promoting. I moved to get radio interviews, posters, and more to promote the business. My cousin Fantasia had a reality show. Teeny, her brother, brought the camera crew to the hair salon.

After those successes, I got deep into promotion and management. My son met some boys that were talented while he was in middle school. He told me that I should sign them. I reached out and talked with them and their parents. I wanted to get them noticed and heard. I had them doing teenage parties and shows. I did pretty good for my first time.

From Highschool to Prison

I came up with a reality show called celebrity managers. I reached out to managers I knew. A woman I knew that produced the R Kelly expose agreed to help. Ten managers responded including Rick Ross' manager. Kevin Hart's manager, Katt Williams' manager, Gary Owen's road manager, Fetty Wap's manager, and several others. We shopped it in Los Angeles. Well, she did. She told me that no one bit on it.

From Highschool to Prison

The managers are the ones who put their lives on hold for the artists. They have wives and husbands, children, and responsibilities. I learned about them as I promoted shows. They do not get the credit they deserve.

Recording Time

I was searching for artists for my record label. I worked a management contract with him. He was noticed instantly. I was more experienced, had more money, and more connections. He started with 400 followers and shot to 5000 in less than 3 months. I got him on deck with social media outlets that promote hip hop. He recorded a song named "Officer" during the George Floyd situation. His video made it to BET Jams. Jamie Foxx shouted him out and became a follower on his Instagram. We ended up doing a song with a cornerback from the Philadelphia Eagles.

I did shows from the east coast to the west coast. Big names like Nikki Minaj and Meek Mills. I had a promotion team and silent investors. We staffed NBA all-star game in New York. We staffed the

Mayweather- Pacquiao fight. CIAA was also ours in Charlotte for several years.

I learned that I am a master marketer and promoter. As I found my ability, I began to think about managing my own artist. I always wanted to start a record label. I never pursued it, but finally got into years later. It was official in 2019. I began with Dollars and Cents Entertainment back before the promotion, but I made it official in 2019 as Carolina Millionaires Entertainment.

From Highschool to Prison

Keep on Trucking

2018, I took my cousin's lead and started trucking school. I started I went to truck driving school and trained for a month. After the training from the company, they wanted to hire me. My point is that you do not always have to have the money to get the training or experience you need. Companies will pay you and train you to do the jobs they want done.

I ran my own trucking company for a year. I had some issues. I went back to work with the company I started with. Some people think that having a felony excludes you from opportunities. It may keep some away from you, but you have several others. Trucking is just one. You can travel the country, make your money, and reflect. While driving, the peace allowed me to think of so many ideas. By law, you must stop for downtime after eleven hours of work. I turned the radio off while I was driving. I was alone with my own thoughts, just me and my truck. I listened to audio books, inspirational talks, lessons, and more.

From Highschool to Prison

I remember I went out to California on a drive in my rig—free trip out from the Carolinas. My best friend's dad manages Kevin Hart. I was able to get front row seats to Kevin's show in Irvine CA. Paid trip. Hooked up seats. All because I found and embraced that there was more to life than just the felony.

From Highschool to Prison

From Highschool to Prison

From Highschool to Prison

From Highschool to Prison

Chapter 11: Investment in People

Surround yourself with people who are doing what you want to do. You may have them in your family, but you must search them out and sit them down and ask about them. Don't get caught up in what you see in the streets.

Some people come home with parole. I am from South Carolina and got in trouble in North Carolina. I had people calling attempting to see what I was up to. People were calling me from South Carolina attempting to throw me some work. They had the mentality that they were looking out for me. But truly, it was a stumbling block to get me back in the pin. I had to keep my guard up. They had not sent money when I was in prison. They did not visit. But they were "looking out for me" when I got out.

As much as you may be talked about, you must endure and embrace the change. "You're acting different. You changed!" They didn't go through what you went through. They do not know the depth of your evolution. You are not required to let them know, but they will see as you remain consistent. They only know you from the person they saw before you left. When you let them know through your actions, they will see.

It may be a challenge at first. Some who looked up to you may not look up to you in the same way. But I found that people that admired me as a cutup, saw my transformation, and were inspired to get out the streets, start businesses, and take better care of their families. I did not go out and preach. I just showed them through my example.

I remember a girl reached out to me on Facebook. She knew me from high school. "You went to prison and came out 8 years later surpassing most of these people you left behind." She went on to tell me that she was proud of me. She congratulated me as a role model and an inspiration. Up to that point, I had not thought of myself in that way. That is my main reason for wanting to speak out publicly. I want to provide another option for people.

Giving Back

When I was 16, on my birthday, I had a cookout in my neighborhood. I do not drink or smoke, but I went and bought all the beer and food for people in the neighborhood to party. I just wanted people to have a good time. When I went back to my hometown, I provided a kid's day event for all the kids. Everything was free. Food,

From Highschool to Prison

games, bouncy houses, and more. I fed and gave money to the community. I paid for free oil changes, bouncy house activities, and more. It was no longer alcohol and intoxication and distraction. It was positives, recreation, and community building.

I remember I also treated all the honor roll kids to Pizza Hut. All the kids in my hometown who made honor roll came to Pizza Hut and ate all they could eat. I want to continue to do things like that.

The point is to give back, but bigger than that, my action is confirmation to parents and children that they can overcome the temptations and deficits of the neighborhood. Too many young men were being killed in my hometown. I wanted to change the vibration—the black cloud—that was over our hood. I wanted people to see that even with some setbacks, mistakes, or deficits they can overcome. It was something to do, but also a positive reality to look on and build from. We made the paper. I cannot say whether I saved lives or not, but I will continue to make my contribution to my community and others.

I had a few people reaching out to me and telling me that they were inspired by my story. It feels good to know that people are inspired by my actions and my ambition. You may be in a crowd and speak to thousands of people. Even one person motivated to change is a positive.

Finding Inspiration

The store owner may be able to tell you how to start a business. Get the information and knowledge. Ask questions and learn. Being in entertainment, my approach has been to supplement what I can do with celebrities that are known by those I want to reach.

I remember a concert we did with local artists and some bigger names. We rented out the civic center near Christmas time to showcase talent and build positive family activities. The goal is always to provide a counterpoint to the negatives the kids experience every day. I also want them to know that someone is watching and noticing that they are working. With the honor roll program, kids may not have known that someone beyond their parents were paying attention. They may have been inspired to go harder and stay consistent because the community is watching.

From Highschool to Prison

With the park event, I wanted to showcase the positives of community. It is not all about death, shooting, and drug sales. Giving back is not only through money. I want to provide a different perspective and be the example that I did not have when I was growing up.

I never saw people donating, encouraging, or advancing with a sense of giving back. I saw people existing and surviving. No one seemed to have the time and perspective to make pathways straight and narrow.

My focus is on the young and the old. I seek to inspire the youth and take care of the old. Young people look up to the drug dealer or the rapper naturally. They may not know that the businessman can do the same thing. I want to show them the lifestyle similarities and the differences. I want to show them that the same money can be used by the drug dealer or the businessman. Both can go to the jewelry store or the car lot buy a flashy car. Either can go to the bank, pull out money, and hold it to their ear. The difference is that the businessman does not need to worry about being raided, his door kicked in, or his family in danger. Money does not need to be blood money. You can get the same money through credit, hard work, and implementation of your ideas. Everyone is chasing the bag, but they have not been taught that they are the bag. Everything you want out of life is accessed through your social security number. You just need to know how to use it.

Herald-Advocate, Bennettsville, S.C. 29512, Thursday, July 7, 2016 - 11

At recent kids day event

Ronnie Hicks helps youth by hosting event

Ronnie Hicks felt that in this county, where he was raised, he had to do something to shift the minds of the children from hearing and seeing so much negativity by bringing something fun, exciting and positive for them. That's when he came up with doing a kids day event on Sat., June 25, dedicated to showing love to the kids in his hometown.

He wanted the community to be involved by donating and volunteering to make the event be a success.

The entire event was free for everyone. The kids ate all they wanted, had all the drinks they wanted, played on bouncy houses for free, won money for racing, and won money from a cash drawing.

They gave a free car wash to a lucky parent and a few free oil changes as well.

Hicks hopes to get more people in the community involved to keep positive activities going on for the young kids.

He is looking forward to making this an annual event for the kids, but will need the support from the community as well. Maybe this event can have the kids looking forward to getting out of school for the summer each year to come out and enjoy a day of fun and all you can eat for free at the kids day event.

From Highschool to Prison

From Highschool to Prison

From Highschool to Prison

From Highschool to Prison

From Highschool to Prison

From Highschool to Prison

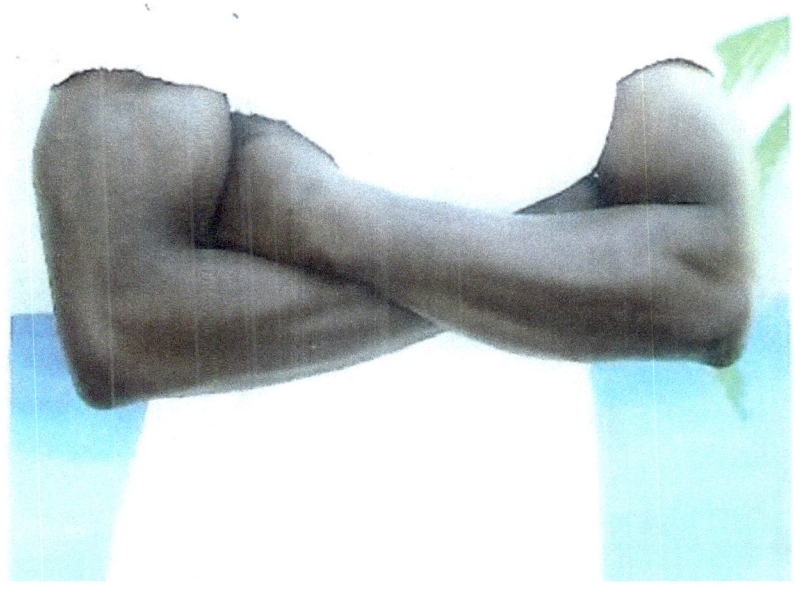

From Highschool to Prison

From Highschool to Prison

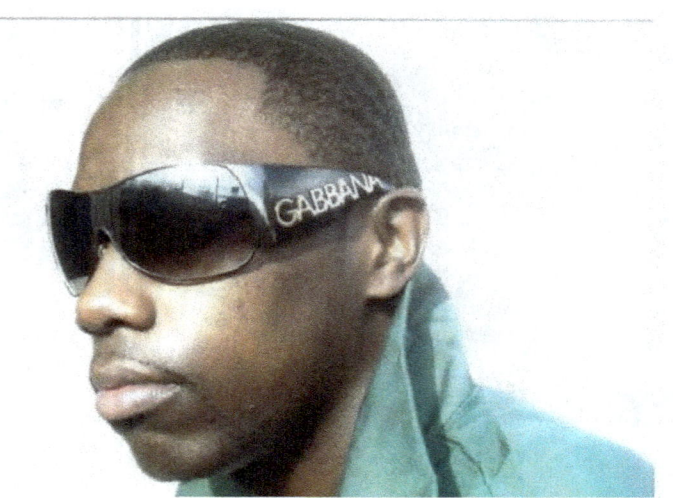

From Highschool to Prison

From Highschool to Prison

From Highschool to Prison

From Highschool to Prison

words'."

Plato said she was able to sit down backstage and visit with Fantasia.

"She said she'd never forget where she came from and the people that put her there," she reported. "She said to tell everybody to keep her in their prayers and she loves them."

BROADWAY STAR - American Idol winner Fantasia Barrineau (left) visits with her cousin Corrie Hicks Plato (center) of Bennettsville and grandmother Addie Collins (right) of High Point, NC, after a recent performance in "The Color Purple" on Broadway.

(Photo submitted)

From Highschool to Prison

From Highschool to Prison

From Highschool to Prison

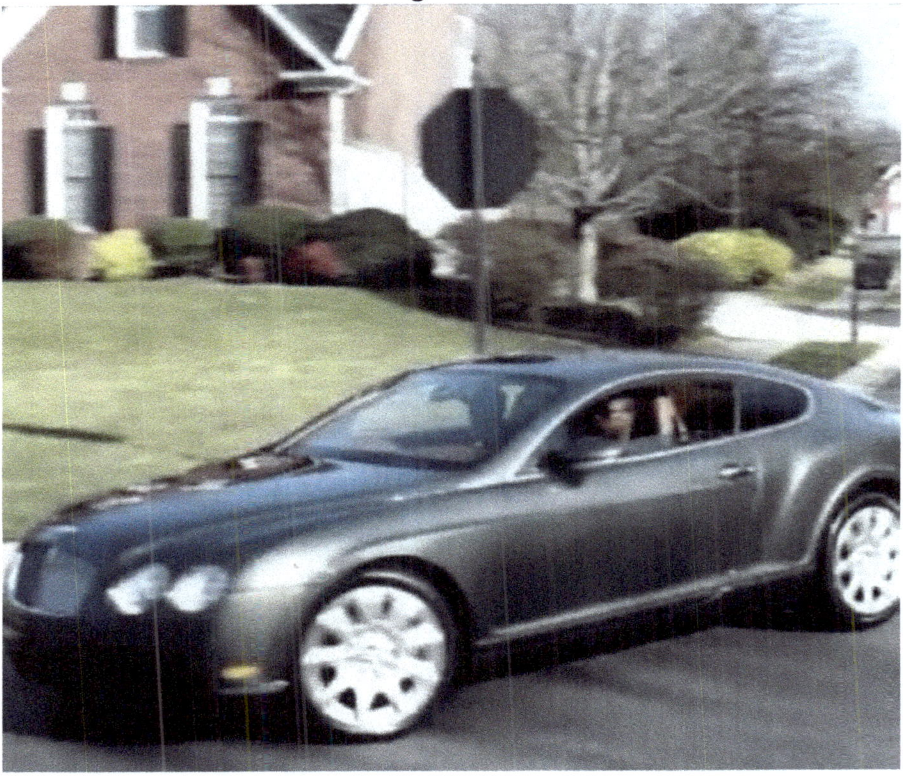

From Highschool to Prison

From Highschool to Prison

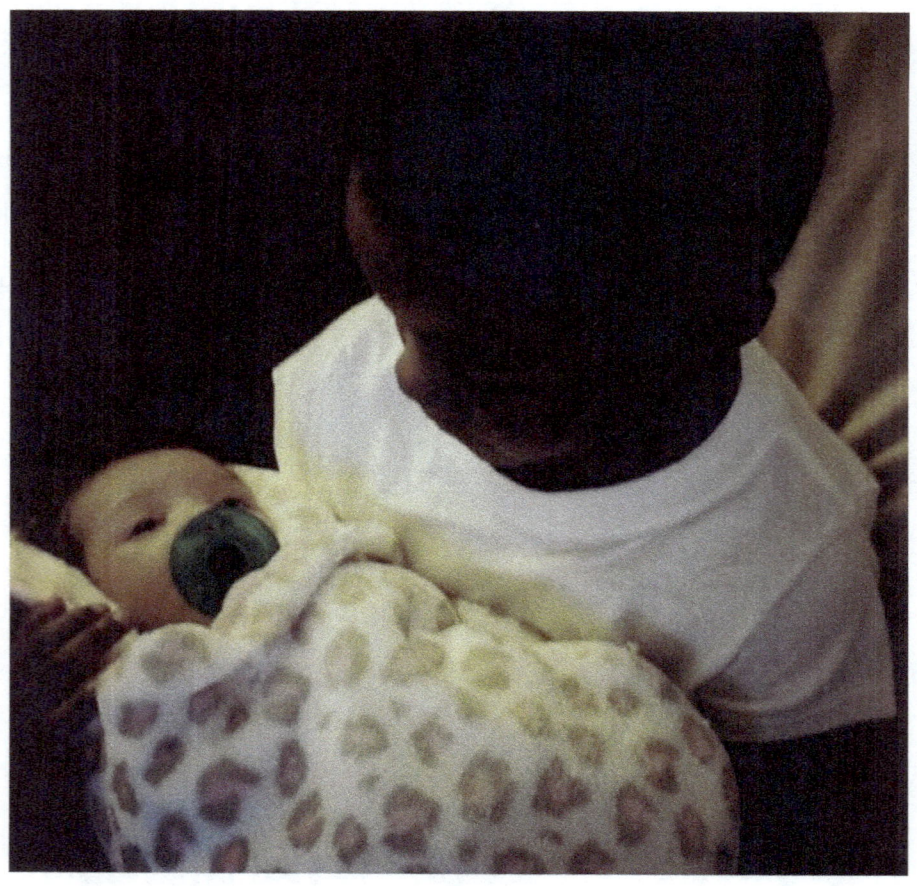

From Highschool to Prison

From Highschool to Prison

From Highschool to Prison

From Highschool to Prison

From Highschool to Prison

Clio Elementary/Middle School announces honor roll lists

Clio Elementary/Middle School recently announced its President's List and A/B honor roll list:

President's List
1st Grade
Andrea Sprattling, Darian O'Neil, Kalia Thomas, and Kayla Woods.
3rd Grade
Kierra Welch and Qui'asha Brown.
5th Grade
Rhonda Bridges and Aliyah McLaughlin.

Kendall Woods
A/B Honor Roll
1st Grade
Tatierra Alford, Shy'Tisha Evans, Quan'Daveon McCollum, Tyrone Alford, Thed Bostic, and Jontavius Loyd.
2nd Grade
Shaliek Hailey, Alexus Quick, Khasiya Sellers, TyQasha Sellers, Taylor Simmons, Janaisa Townsend, Joshua Woods, Ron-Quisha McRae, Da'Quesha Wilson, TyDasha Sellers, Jacqueline Oney, and Christopher Brown.

3rd Grade
Kyla Thomas, Kierra Welch, and Jordan Bennett.
4th Grade
London Johnson, Deja McQueen, Jasmine Loyc, and Jean'ae Teal.
5th Grade
Tavares Adams, Maisha Jacobs, Malik Miles, Keyona Johnson, and Holly Smith.
6th Grade
Brian Stuckey.
7th Grade
Jamie Polston.
8th Grade
April Bethea.

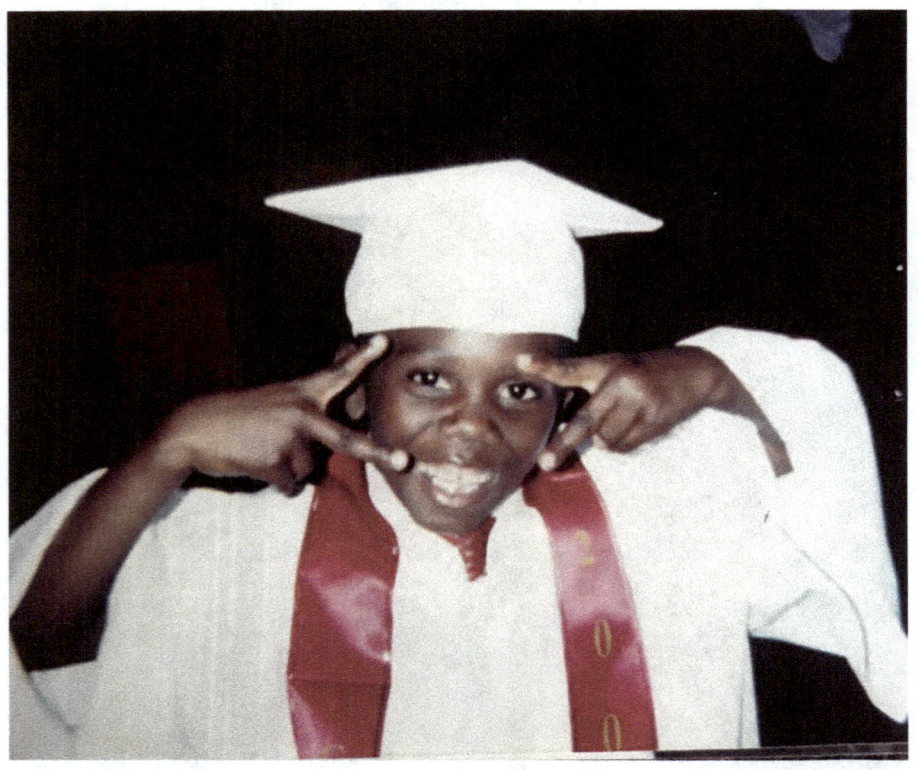

From Highschool to Prison

From Highschool to Prison

From Highschool to Prison

From Highschool to Prison

Nicki Minaj & Meek Mill Ciaa Weekend Oasis Tent 2015

7.1K views

43   0   Share   Download   Save

 CarolinaMillionairesEnt.   **SUBSCRIBE**

From Highschool to Prison

From Highschool to Prison

From Highschool to Prison

From Highschool to Prison

From Highschool to Prison

From Highschool to Prison

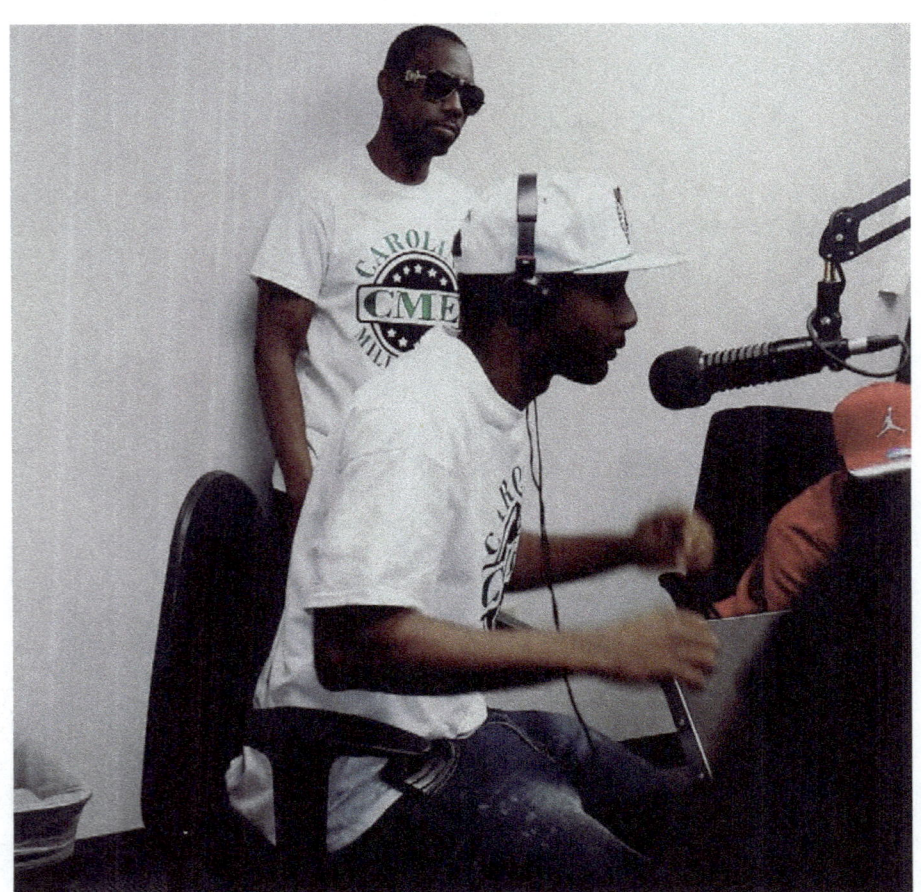

From Highschool to Prison

From Highschool to Prison

From Highschool to Prison

From Highschool to Prison

From Highschool to Prison

From Highschool to Prison

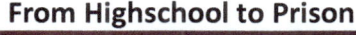

From Highschool to Prison

From Highschool to Prison

From Highschool to Prison

From Highschool to Prison

From Highschool to Prison

From Highschool to Prison

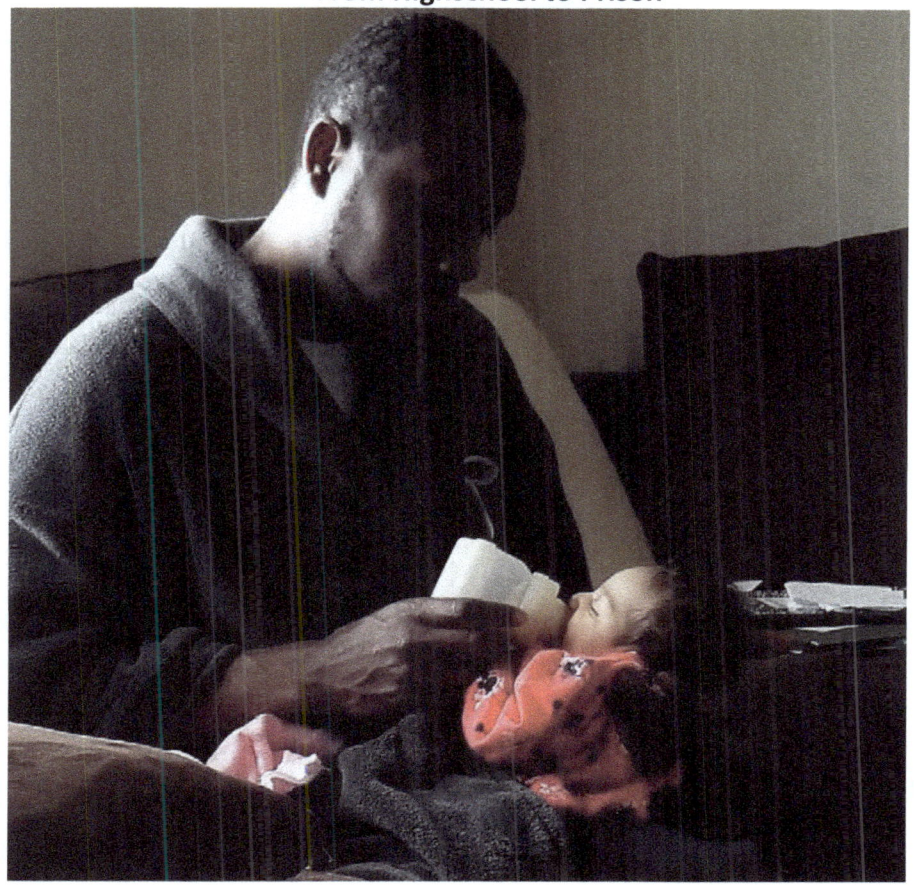

From Highschool to Prison

From Highschool to Prison

From Highschool to Prison

From Highschool to Prison

From Highschool to Prison

From Highschool to Prison

From Highschool to Prison

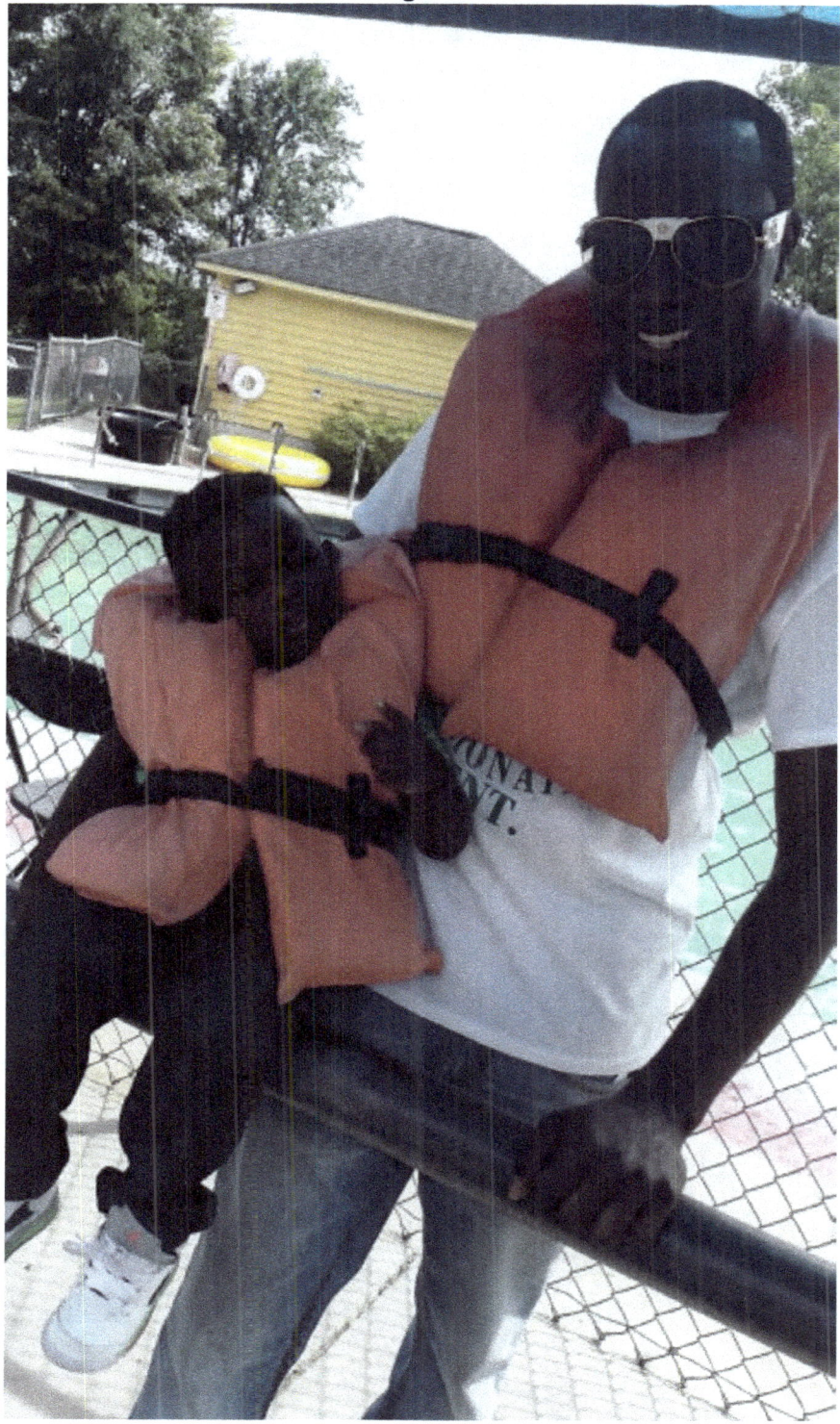

From Highschool to Prison

www.ingramcontent.com/pod-product-compliance
Lightning Source LLC
Chambersburg PA
CBHW070916180426
43192CB00037B/1368